Publication Number 21

Duke University Commonwealth-Studies Center

**Bureaucratic Transition
in Malaya**

Duke University Commonwealth-Studies Center Publications

1. *The British Commonwealth: An Experiment in Co-operation among Nations*, by Frank H. Underhill   2. *South Africa: Economic and Political Aspects*, by Hector Menteith Robertson   3. *Some Comparative Aspects of Irish Law*, by Alfred Gaston Donaldson   4. *Economic Analysis and Policy in Underdeveloped Countries*, by P. T. Bauer   5. *The Higher Public Service of the Commonwealth of Australia*, by Howard A. Scarrow   6. *Economic Opinion and Policy in Ceylon*, by Henry M. Oliver, Jr.   7. *Problems of the New Commonwealth*, by Sir Ivor Jennings   8. *Commonwealth Perspectives*, by Nicholas Mansergh, *et al.*   9. *Evolving Canadian Federalism*, by A. R. M. Lower, F. R. Scott, *et al.*   10. *The Commonwealth Economy in Southeast Asia*, by T. H. Silcock   11. *Public Expenditures in Australia*, by B. U. Ratchford   12. *The American Economic Impact on Canada*, by Hugh G. J. Aitken, John J. Deutsch, W. A. Mackintosh, *et al.*   13. *Tradition, Values, and Socio-Economic Development*, edited by Ralph Braibanti and Joseph J. Spengler   14. *The Growth of Canadian Policies in External Affairs*, by Hugh L. Keenleyside, *et al.*   15. *Canadian Economic Thought: The Political Economy of a Developing Nation 1814–1914*, by Craufurd D. W. Goodwin   16. *Economic Systems of the Commonwealth*, edited by Calvin B. Hoover   17. *The Nigerian Political Scene*, edited by Robert O. Tilman and Taylor Cole   18. *Administration and Economic Development in India*, edited by Ralph Braibanti and Joseph J. Spengler   19. *Canada–United States Treaty Relations*, edited by David R. Deener   20. *Post-primary Education and Political and Economic Development*, edited by Don C. Piper and Taylor Cole   21. *Bureaucratic Transition in Malaya*, by Robert O. Tilman

Bureaucratic Transition in Malaya

Robert O. Tilman

Published for the
Duke University Commonwealth-Studies Center
Duke University Press, Durham, N.C.
Cambridge University Press, London
1964

© 1964, Duke University Press

Library of Congress Catalogue Card number 64-20418
Cambridge University Press, London N.W. 1, England

Printed in the United States of America
by Vail-Ballou Press, Inc., Binghamton, N.Y.

Preface

The Federation of Malaya achieved political independence on August 31, 1957, and became absorbed into the greater Federation of Malaysia on September 16, 1963. Although the life span of the original Federation was only a brief six years and fifteen days, the period saw dramatic changes in the peninsula. Emergency operations against communist insurgency came to an official and successful close in July, 1960; social and educational development was proceeding at a pace unimagined during the colonial period; economic expansion and diversification was impressive; and— perhaps most important—the parliamentary system of government, introduced in stages during the colonial regime, was still functioning and was providing Malaya with one of the most stable political systems in Southeast Asia.

Within this framework of parliamentary government was also to be found one of the most effective and efficient bureaucracies in the area, a fact that in no small measure accounted for the Federation's success in executing its ambitious development plans. Moreover, by the time of the creation of the greater Malaysian Federation this bureaucracy was largely indigenous in composition, and the few remaining European colonial servants were working side by side with locally recruited officers and recently arrived foreign advisers. These happy circumstances were not entirely accidental, nor were they exclusively a product of the period of political independence. As this monograph will attempt to demonstrate, modern Malayan bureaucracy is a synthesis of the colonial experience as it acted, reacted, and interacted within the indigenous environment of a tropical, plural, Southeast Asian society. The attempt will be made here to trace this transitional process from the arrival of the agents of British colonialism to the emergence of the Malayan synthesis as it existed at the time of the creation of the Federation of Malaysia.

Material for the present study was gathered in the course of several visits to Malaya and London during the period 1959–63. This research was made possible by grants from the Duke University Commonwealth-Studies Center and the Social Science Research Council, without whose support the present monograph would have been impossible. While the author is indebted to these organizations for the opportunity of undertaking this project, it should perhaps be pointed out that the material presented here in no way reflects the views or policies of either group.

During the years that this research was underway the author also became indebted to numerous individuals without whose assistance the gathering of material would have been considerably more difficult, if not impossible. The Government of the Federation of Malaya extended its official co-operation to the maximum limits possible commensurate with the demands of the national interests, and individual members of the bureaucracy devoted many hours of their valuable time to providing information. Omitting far more names than can be included, I am particularly indebted to Dato Abdul Aziz bin Haji Abdul Majid, Permanent Secretary, Prime Minister's Department; Dato Hamzah bin Abdullah and Mr. C. R. Howitt, Chairman and Deputy Chairman respectively of the Public Services Commission; and to the Principal Assistant Secretaries and others in the Federation Establishment Office, particularly the former PAS (Establishments), Mr. A. R. Mann, who not only was a constant source of information but who also undertook the laborious task of reading a very early draft of the present study. Occasionally the analysis and observations presented here may not be in agreement with the views of the individuals who provided the information, and such differences of opinion often came out in the course of personal conversations; however, I have tried throughout the study to present a detached and objective view of Malayan bureaucracy (a neutral term that was itself often a source of irritation to Malayan and British acquaintances). I hope that this desire for objectivity will be appreciated by my many friends throughout the government though they may not always agree with my conclusions.

I am also greatly indebted to a number of academicians and former Malayan government officials who have undertaken to provide editorial comment at various stages in the manuscript. Sir David Watherston, the last Federal Secretary of pre-independent Malaya, graciously agreed to read and criticize Chapters II–V; Mr. J. M. Gullick provided detailed comments on Chapter I; and Professor T. H. Silcock, Professor Emeritus of Economics at the University of Singapore, read and criticized the entire manuscript. Though I have not always accepted the advice of these critics, many of the suggested changes have been incorporated into the present version, and I am certain that it is now a better monograph because of their assistance. I am also indebted to Professors Ralph Braibanti and R. Taylor Cole of Duke University. This project was formulated and executed under the general direction of Professor Braibanti, whose advice has proved invaluable. Although Professor Cole was not directly involved in the collection or analysis of this material, frequent association with him over a two-year period proved a constant source of inspiration and undoubtedly influenced the character of the study. While these, and numerous others as well, have contributed to the final product, they cannot be blamed for any errors of omission or commission; these are the author's alone.

Finally, I must record my appreciation for a tolerant wife, who has had the pleasant experience of two visits to Malaya, but who has also had to listen to far more discussions of Malayan bureaucracy than should be expected of any wife.

R. O. T.

Tulane University, September 19, 1963

Contents

1. The Malayan Environment   3

    I. The Traditional Socio-Economic Order   4

    II. The Plural Nature of Malayan Society   16

    III. The Origins and Effects of Social Heterogeneity   25

2. Colonial Bureaucracy and the Malayan Colonial Experience   37

    I. Malayan Bureaucracy under Company Rule   37

    II. The Colonial Office Period of Malayan Administrative History   45

    III. The Role of the Colonial Bureaucracy in Malayan Development   49

    IV. Conclusion   60

3. The Transitional Phase   63

    I. The Malayanization Scheme   63

    II. The Statistical Results of Malayanization   68

    III. The Complications of Malayanization   77

4. The Institutional Legacy   82

    I. The Formal Organization of the Federal Bureaucracy   84

    II. Internal Administration of the Bureaucracy   90

5. The Administrative Legacy   102

    I. The Position of the MCS in the Bureaucratic Hierarchy   102

    II. The MCS and the ICS: Continuity and Discontinuity   104

    III. The Character of the Contemporary MCS   107

IV. Conclusion: The Administrative Services and the
Political Process   115

6. Malayan Bureaucracy: The Process of Change and the Future   121

I. Bureaucracy in Transition: The Broad Perspective   121

II. Bureaucracy in Transition: The Future   132

III. Bureaucracy in Transition: A Summation   137

Appendixes

A. Questionnaire for Writers Receiving Appointments in
the Service of the East India Company   141

B. Agreements for the Constitution of a Federation
Establishment   142

C. Constitution of the Federation of Malaya, Part X:
The Public Services   145

A Selected Bibliography of Public Documents Relating to Malayan Bureaucracy   159

Index   173

Tables

1. Malaya: Communal Composition, 1921–57   16
2. Malaya: Population Projections, by Community, 1957–82   17
3. Malaya: Geographic Distribution of Population, by
   Community, 1957   18
4. Malaya: Communal Composition of Urban Population, 1947–
   57, by Percentages   18
5. Malaya: Percentage of Total Population of Each Community
   Living in Urban Centers, by State   19
6. Literacy Rates, 10 Years of Age and Over, by
   Community and Language, 1957, in Percentages   20
7. Malaya: Economically Active Population, by Community and
   Industry Divisions in Percentages   23
8. FMS: Tin Production, 1896–1957   51
9. FMS: Rubber Production, 1906–53   53
10. FMS: Sources of Revenue, 1896–1936, M\$ Millions   54
11. Railway Mileage, Pan-Malayan, 1902–39   56
12. FMS: Growth of Selected Services, 1913–32   57
13. FMS: Telephone and Telegraph Service, 1903–35   58
14. FMS: Government and Government-Aided Schools, 1891–
   1936   59
15. FMS: Distribution of Schools, 1921, According to Language
   of Instruction   60
16. The Malayanization of the Senior Bureaucracy, 1956–62   68
17. Communal Representation in the Senior Bureaucracy,
   1957–62   70
18. Total Non-European Senior Bureaucracy: Comparative
   Recruitment by Communities, 1957 and 1962   71
19. Total Non-European Senior Bureaucracy, Less Medical
   Services, 1957 and 1962   72
20. Malayan Civil Service, by Community, 1957–62   73
21. Medical Services, by Community, 1957–62   73
22. Police Services, by Community, 1957–62   73
23. Education Services, by Community, 1957–62   73

24. Public Works Department Services, by Community, 1957–62   74
25. Bureaucracy Requiring General Educational Background
    (Category One), by Community, 1957–62   75
26. Technical and Professional Bureaucracy: Scientific
    Background (Category Two), by Community, 1957–62   75
27. Technical and Professional Bureaucracy: Non-Scientific
    Background (Category Three), by Community, 1957–62   75
28. Non-Professional Bureaucracy (Category Four), by
    Community, 1957–62   75
29. Federal Bureaucracy, by Division and Ministry   85
30. Total Bureaucracy. by State and Total Federal   86
31. Elected and Party Elite: Avenues of Recruitment   116

Graphs

1. The Malayanization of the Senior Bureaucracy   70
2. Structure of Selected Division I Services   103

Bureaucratic Transition
in Malaya

The Malayan Environment

Contemporary Malayan bureaucracy must be viewed as a product of the total Malayan environment, for its development has been influenced by the culture, history, and politics of Hinduized, Islamic, colonial, and independent Malaya. To be sure, the present bureaucratic structure has been disproportionately affected by the colonial experience—and thus the colonial bureaucracy must be considered in later chapters in a more thorough manner— but this bureaucracy must function in a society, and be influenced by a society, that has roots extending through the four major eras of Malayan history. These eras have each introduced innovations that have affected the nature of the present social and political organization and thus deserve at least cursory attention before a more careful examination of the bureaucracy itself can be undertaken. It is the purpose of this introductory chapter to explore this historical, social, and political environment, though it is probably unnecessary to point out that the choice of subjects must be limited to those that seem most directly related to the development of the present bureaucratic machine. Over a long period of history cause and effect become hopelessly intertwined, and attempts to isolate causal influences are complex and sometimes frustrating exercises. Nevertheless, it does seem possible at least to divide our subject into two broad categories, each of which exhibits a lingering influence on the nature of the bureaucratic system. Part one of this chapter will therefore deal with the nature of pre-European Malaya, while parts two and three will discuss some particular influences of the social system that have roots in the more recent colonial past.

I. The Traditional Socio-Economic Order

To talk about a traditional socio-economic order suggests immediately a dichotomy between "tradition" and "modernity"—a dichotomy that may seem self-evident, but one that is nevertheless difficult to define.[1] In a sense, we are always culture-bound, for almost any definition of modernity, upon close analysis, reveals it to be a description of an ideal abstraction based on the society in which we are now living. Accepting this cultural limitation, and accepting that these conceptualizations may be on the same continuum, they nevertheless seem separated by sufficient distance to make the terms meaningful in social and political analysis. Many social scientists are in agreement that modern societies are characterized by a high degree of social mobility based on achievemental factors, widespread participation in mass media of communications, a concomitantly high literacy rate, a social system exhibiting a high degree of functional differentiation, a rational ordering of the economic system that maximizes efficiency, and widespread urbanization. Admittedly, this is an abstraction, for no actual society has ever fully satisfied these criteria. However, just as this is the "Platonic form" of the modern society, so the opposite would be the ideal type of the traditional society. The characteristics of the latter would be a fixed social stratification based on ascriptive factors, restricted participation in the communications process, a concomitantly low

1. The author here is generally following the sociological tradition of Sir Henry Maine, Ferdinand Tönnies, Max Weber, and Robert Redfield, among others. I am particularly indebted to the work of contemporary scholars in the field of comparative politics, such as Fred W. Riggs, Gabriel A. Almond, James S. Coleman, Lucian W. Pye, and, a sociologist, Daniel Lerner. See especially Professor Riggs's "Agraria and Industria," in William J. Siffin, ed., *Toward the Comparative Study of Public Administration* (Bloomington, Indiana: Indiana University Press, 1959); *The Ecology of Public Administration* (London: Asia Publishing House, 1961); and "An Ecological Approach—The 'Sala' Model," a paper presented at the Annual Meeting of the American Political Science Association (St. Louis, September 6–9, 1961). Also see Daniel Lerner, *The Passing of Traditional Society* (Glencoe, Ill.: The Free Press, 1958), *passim*, esp. pp. 43–75; Gabriel A. Almond and James S. Coleman, eds., *The Politics of the Developing Areas* (Princeton: Princeton University Press, 1960), pp. 3–64, 532–76; and Lucian W. Pye, *Politics, Personality, and Nation Building* (New Haven and London: Yale University Press, 1962), pp. 32–56.

literacy rate, a highly undifferentiated socio-political system, a non-rational economic system with a highly unfavorable input-output ratio, and a widely dispersed rural population, or perhaps a population located in a conglomeration of villages, the organization of each constituting a microcosmic duplication of the ordering of the total society. The goal of the traditional society was stability and order, not innovation and change. Society was corporate, not individualistic. The rights of man *qua* man was a doctrine that was largely beyond comprehension. The emphasis was on obligations and duties, not on rights and privileges. The rights of individuals were those that were derived from obligations to the total society.

Again, it must be pointed out that this description is an abstraction, and undoubtedly its actual counterpart is not to be found in historical chronicles. That societies do not conform to these dichotomous models has led some social scientists, particularly those interested in the comparative study of the phenomena of political change, to seek hypothetical constructs that might be employed to analyze actual political systems in terms of their combined "traditional" and "modern" characteristics. Though the range of agreement on precise techniques and methods is still restricted, careful work by social scientists such as Fred Riggs, Ralph Braibanti, and Lucian Pye suggests that the tradition-modernity spectrum has both validity and utility.[2] Evidence in Malaya supports this conclusion, for only when adequate account is taken of the continuing influence of tradition does the political process, including the development and the role of the bureaucracy, become intelligible.

2. Riggs, in the sources cited above, has made the most concerted and consistent attempts to construct models useful for analyzing bureaucracies in a state of transition. David Apter has provided some brilliant insights into the political process in the new states, but his research focuses less on bureaucracy and bureaucratic change than does that of Riggs. (See David Apter, "Comprehensive Method for the Study of Politics," *The American Journal of Sociology*, LXIV [Nov., 1958], 221–37; *The Gold Coast in Transition* [Princeton: Princeton University Press, 1955]; and *The Political Kingdom in Uganda* [Princeton: Princeton University Press, 1961]. For an incisive analysis of the basic issues facing students of political change, see Ralph Braibanti, "The Relevance of Political Science to the Study of the Underdeveloped Areas," in Ralph Braibanti and J. J. Spengler, eds., *Traditions, Values, and Socio-Economic Development* [Durham, N.C.: Duke University Press, 1961], pp. 139–80.)

(1) *Malayan Tradition: History and Sources*

Attention in this section will be devoted primarily to a political analysis of the Malacca Sultanate and Islamic political orders based on or derived from the Malacca Sultanate,[3] but it should be understood that Malaya has been subjected not to one but to several traditions. Thus, even when discussing the ancient Muslim political and social order, the subject represents a homogenization of Shaman, Siva, and Sufi—to borrow a title by Sir Richard O. Winstedt.[4] Malaya was subjected to succeeding invasions, first by the Hindus—beginning as early as the opening centuries of the Christian era—and then by the Muslims, when the culture radiated from the Malacca Sultanate, which was created about 1400 and continued until the Portuguese invasion of Malacca in 1511.[5]

3. Malacca was the first indigenous political system of Malaya that integrated a population larger than a village or district, and the Malacca Sultanate was the center from which Islam was diffused throughout the Archipelago. (D. G. E. Hall, *A History of South-East Asia* [London: Macmillan and Co. Ltd., 1958], p. 198; and J. M. Gullick, *Indigenous Political Systems of Western Malaya* [London: Athlone Press, 1958], p. 7.) Most important for the purposes of this essay, Malacca was the source of the tradition and patterns of political organization inherited by the other Malay States of the Peninsula. There is also a direct historical connection since the last Malacca Sultan became the ruler of Johore and thereby assumed hegemony over the Malay States south of Siam. (C. D. Cowan, *Nineteenth-Century Malaya* [London: Oxford University Press, 1961], p. 5.)

4. *Shaman, Saiva and Sufi* (London: Constable and Co. Ltd., 1925). For the second edition, see *The Malay Magician: Being Shaman, Saiva and Sufi* (London: Routledge and Kegan Paul, 1951).

5. The standard works on early Indian and Muslim influences in Malaya, from which most contemporary accounts must draw heavily, are George Coédes, *Les États Hindouisés d'Indochine et d'Indonésie* (Paris: E. de Boccard, 1948); and Tomé Pires (trans. by A. Cortesão), *Suma Oriental* (2 vols.; London: Hakluyt Society, 1944). The major secondary works on this early period are Sir Richard O. Winstedt, "A History of Malaya," originally published as a regular number of the *Journal of the Malayan Branch of the Royal Asiatic Society*, XIII (March, 1935); and Winstedt's briefer and more popular treatment, *Malaya and Its History* (London: Hutchinson's University Library, 1951). Also see Hall, chaps. ii–iv, x; J. Kennedy, *A History of Malaya, A.D. 1400–1959* (London: Macmillan and Co. Ltd., 1962), chap. i; and F. J. Moorhead, *A History of Malaya and Her Neighbours* (London: Longmans, Green and Co. Ltd., 1957), Vol. I, chaps. iii–vii. A useful primary source dealing with the Malacca Sultanate is *Sejarah Melayu* (*The Malay Annals*). The most recent translation is by C. C. Brown and appeared as parts 2 and 3 of Vol. XXV, *Journal of the Malayan Branch of the Royal Asiatic Society* (Oct., 1952). One of the most famous translations, which contains an introduction by Thomas S. (later Sir Stamford) Raffles, is John Leyden, trans., *Malay Annals* (London: Longman, Hurst, Rees, Orme and Brown, 1821). *The Annals*, which contains a liberal sprinkling of fancy interlaced with many accepted facts, was probably written by a man who lived through the Portuguese capture of Malacca in 1511, was altered about 1612, and suffered various interpolations after that date. (See Sir Richard O. Winstedt, "The Malay Annals or *Sejarah Melayu*," *Journal*

Although the story of the Malacca Sultanate has now been adequately reconstructed in terms of personalities and historical events, remarkably little attention has been given to careful analyses of the regime's social and political organization. The following pages have been drawn together from the sources cited above and—where seemingly applicable—from analyses of traditional Hindu political systems of the Indian Subcontinent.[6] Thus, while an adequate account can be assembled, the story may appear more coherent and complete than it actually is: many of the generalizations presented must be regarded only as tentative hypotheses at the present time.

(2) *Ascriptive Nature of Political Legitimacy*

The ascriptive political hierarchy of pre-European Malaya was capped by the Malay Sultan, a position that combined social prestige and religious authority with a modicum of real political power. The Sultan was the symbol of Muslim unity, and—as the reference point from which social distance was measured—he provided the absolute standard on which status in the social system could be judged.[7] While largely symbolic, the Sultan never-

of the Malayan Branch of the Royal Asiatic Society, XVI [Dec., 1938], 1–26.)
Gullick, in the study cited in n. 3, provides one of the most useful accounts dealing primarily with the organization and personalities of government in the pre-European period. For a fuller listing of secondary source material on this period, see the appropriate citations in H. R. Cheeseman, comp., *Bibliography of Malaya* (London: Longmans, Green and Co., 1959), pp. 78–104. Most histories of Malaya have tended to be Eurocentric, though the pioneering work of men such as Winstedt and Gullick has helped to right the imbalance.

6. Here I am particularly indebted to Gullick, *op. cit.* This monograph is based primarily on the experiences of Perak, Selangor, and Negri Sembilan and is drawn chiefly from early accounts by British administrators that described the indigenous systems; thus, when using this material to support generalizations that might be applicable to the Malacca Sultanate and later political systems, certain assumptions must be made that are actually very tenuous. J. M. Gullick, in a personal communication to the author (May 12, 1963) puts forward the view that his *Indigenous Political Systems of Western Malaya* should be regarded as purely and explicitly nineteenth-century material. Though I have tried to exercise some caution in employing such assumptions, the reader nevertheless deserves to be reminded that some of these conclusions may be subject to revision and refinement in light of later research. The most useful source dealing with traditional Hindu political systems is A. L. Basham, *The Wonder That Was India* (New York: Grove Press, Inc., 1954), chap. iv. Great care has been exercised in basing conclusions on Hindu practice, and only where present-day institutions and ritual clearly reflect Hindu origins has this source been employed.

7. Gullick, p. 66.

theless could often exert some political power, either as a result of the predominance of his personality or in cases where disputes arose among the Sultan's territorial chiefs.[8]

Clustered around the Sultan was a grouping of four concentric circles (or ranks) of *mentris* (ministers) organized on a cosmological principle [9] and numbering a total of probably sixty persons. The relationship of each of the officers to the Sultan became fixed by custom. The offices themselves were generally hereditary, and strict rules emerged for determining the order of succession.

Beneath the social level of the Sultan and his ministers came the territorial chiefs, each ruling over a district, the shape and size of which was largely determined by the geographic configuration of rivers and valleys. Except in rare cases, the District Chiefs really represented the top level of government. While the Sultan's role was largely symbolic and ritualistic, chiefs were primarily concerned with controlling the population encompassed in their areas. The chiefs might have turned toward the Sultan to provide symbolic legitimacy—a practice of some importance, of course, in the development of the later Malay States—but in the end they generally maintained control of their districts through their own wits.[10]

Just as the circle of ministers about the Sultan was hereditary and generally related to the Sultan's family, so too the advisors and administrators clustered around the District Chiefs were kinsmen known for their personal loyalty. The chief provided a

8. *Ibid.*, pp. 69, 97. Historians do not agree on the active role of the Sultan. There is considerable evidence that later Sultans of the Malacca period were content to enjoy the privileges and benefits of their positions without exhibiting great interest in exerting political power. See R. J. Wilkinson, "The Malacca Sultanate," *Journal of the Straits Branch of the Royal Asiatic Society*, No. 61 (June, 1912), p. 70.

9. On the use of cosmological numbers in the political system, see pp. 11 ff below. Technically speaking, the fourth rank of thirty-two did not carry the title of *mentri*.

10. I am indebted to J. M. Gullick (see communication cited in n. 6, above) for pointing out that the relative power of the Sultans varied between the original Malacca Sultanate and the later Sultans who branched off from the early Sultanate. Gullick argues convincingly that Malacca, drawing its revenues from the taxing of international trade that called at the single port, became "a compact system of power in which all the high offices were concentrated at the center." On the other hand, by the middle of the nineteenth century trade was of only minor importance. The wealth of any state was largely dependent upon its tin deposits, which were scattered about outside the royal capitals, and thus the rulers could secure revenue only through the territorial chiefs who governed these rich areas.

lieutenant with a source of livelihood (more often than not the opportunity to extract whatever payments he could secure from his administrative area) and protection; the lieutenant in return maintained control of his area and remitted a portion of the revenues to the District Chief.[11] There were, of course, always challenges to the authority of the chief by discontented lieutenants, and the chief's effectiveness in controlling and manipulating these challenges was the real test of his political acumen.

The smallest political unit of traditional Malaya—and contemporary Malaya as well—was the *kampong*, or village. The *penghulu* (village headman) in district affairs was primarily a servant of the District Chief and his lieutenants. Even in purely local affairs he was less a political decision-maker than might have been the Japanese *burako-chō* or the headman of the Indian village *panchayat*. In the village Council of Elders the *penghulu* was *primus inter pares*, though it seems that the emphasis was more on equality than on primacy. His primary function was to help resolve differences and steer the group toward a consensus. As in Japan and India, the only coercive sanctions in the hands of the Council of Elders were social, but it seems unlikely that these ever became as effective as *mura hachibu* (social ostracism) in Japan or outcasting by the caste *panchayat* in India.

The predominance of an ascriptive ruling class was one of the most significant characteristics of traditional Malay political systems. Vertical social movement into this class was almost impossible, though bridging of this social chasm by intermarriage was possible on rare occasions.[12] Societal norms not only discouraged social ambitions, but traditional stories stressing stability and familiar sayings such as "as is the mold, so will be the cake" made immobility a positive virtue.[13]

Thus, Malayan society, and the political order as well, remained relatively stable in hierarchical status from the emergence of the Malacca Sultanate until the penetration of Europeans, a process

11. Gullick, p. 73. Also see *ibid.*, p. 97.
12. *Ibid.*, pp. 21, 65, 81.
13. C. C. Brown, *Malay Sayings* (London: Routledge and Kegan Paul, 1951), p. 132; also see Sir Richard O. Winstedt, *Malay Proverbs* (London: Murray and Co., 1950), p. 36.

that began in 1511 but gained momentum only in the nineteenth century. To be sure, the social structure was changing, but as Sir Denzil Ibbetson summarized the fluidity of social change in pre-British India:

. . . society is not solid but liquid, and portions of it are continually rising and sinking and changing their position as measured by that scale; and the only real difference . . . is that . . . [Indian society] is much more viscous, the friction and inertia to be overcome infinitely greater, and the movement therefore far slower. . . .[14]

(3) *Religion and Magic in the Traditional Political System*

As in other traditional societies, the Malay Sultan was hedged in divinity, both in his person and in his royal regalia. Upon installation the Sultan underwent a magic change and emerged different from his previous self and different from his kinsmen and followers. Those who violated the majesty of the Sultan would be punished, not necessarily by the Sultan himself, but more likely by the supernatural forces that surrounded his royal person. The Sultan possessed powers superior to those of ordinary mortals and he was able to perpetuate these powers through participation in rites and rituals.[15] The Malay Sultan had the divine power to alter the course of nature, a power that also devolved upon the Sultan's duly appointed representatives.[16]

Not only was the Sultan divine, but the regalia surrounding the Sultan was equally possessed of supernatural powers. The precise pieces of regalia varied from state to state, but generally included such items as the royal umbrella, drums, flutes, betel box, sword, scepter, seal of state, standards, and pennants.[17] The *Malay Annals* abounds with detailed protocol confining to the ruler or his

14. *Panjab Castes* (Lahore: Superintendent, Government Printing, Punjab, 1916), p. 9.
15. Note here the similarity to the position of the traditional Hindu kings. See Basham, p. 81.
16. See Walter William Skeat, *Malay Magic* (London: Macmillan and Co., 1900), pp. 36–37.
17. *Ibid., passim.* Also see Robert Heine-Geldern, "Conceptions of State and Kingship in Southeast Asia," *Data Paper No. 18* (Ithaca, New York: Cornell University Southeast Asia Program, April, 1956, mimeographed).

family the exclusive use of many of these items and prescribing their employment at state functions.[18]

One of the most important items of the royal regalia was the umbrella, still an accepted symbol of sovereignty in contemporary Malaya.[19] According to the *Malay Annals* the appropriate color of the Sultan's umbrella was white, while those of the Sultan's family should be yellow. However, over time the custom was modified—probably beginning in Selangor according to Skeat [20] —to substitute the yellow for the white umbrella and eventually to proscribe the wearing of yellow clothing and ornamentation at official functions for all but the royal person.[21] Regardless of color, the most important function of the umbrella was that it provided the home for a "protective genius who favored the king with his advice and who in critical moments even actively intervened on behalf of the dynasty." [22]

The political system of traditional Malaya was organized on cosmological principles, at least above the level of the District Chiefs. In most states there were four ministers of the first rank, eight of the second rank, sixteen of the third rank, and thirty-two (who technically were not *mentris*) of the fourth rank.[23]

The most powerful and prestigious of the Sultan's ministers was the *Bendahara,* or as it is usually translated, the Prime Minister. The title is Indian in origin, but it seems probable that the *Bendahara's* duties grew largely from indigenous needs. In the absence of the Sultan he could carry out some of the important functions of the state in the name of the ruler, and at the death

18. Chap. xi.
19. At ceremonial functions in the Federation the Yang di-Pertuan Agong is always shaded by a handsome yellow umbrella borne by an attendant.
20. P. 34.
21. The white umbrella is the symbol of sovereignty in Hindu political thought, but it is not certain whether the Malacca Sultanate attributed the custom to Hindu practice or associated it with the colored sides of the mythical Mount Meru (which will be discussed below).
22. Heine-Geldern, p. 9.
23. There are scattered evidences that the cosmological requirement of 4-8-16-32 was not fulfilled in at least one system, but documentary proof is sketchy. It is probable that one major piece of evidence (a report made by an eighteenth-century Dutch official) might have been in error. Similarly, the *Malay Annals* vaguely implies a slightly different ordering, but inaccuracies are not unusual in this source. See Winstedt, *The Malays: A Cultural History,* p. 73.

of a Sultan it was the *Bendahara* who was entrusted with the protection of the royal regalia until a new ruler could be enthroned.[24] Also among the four *mentris* of the first rank were the *Temenggong* (or commander of the troops, a title with Indonesian origins, having also appeared prominently in the Majapahit polity), *Penghulu Bendahari* (treasurer and probably secretary to the Sultan), and *Mentri* (usually translated secretary of state, but the duties of this officer are not adequately understood).[25]

The most important *mentri* of the second rank was probably the *Shahbandar* (collector of port duties), particularly in the bustling port of Malacca during the period of the Sultanate. The *Shahbandar* administered the port according to prescribed regulations in a remarkably just and efficient manner according to Tomé Pires.[26] The remaining titles and duties of the eight *mentris* of the second rank are obscure, though there is some mention of the *Sri Maharaja Lela* (apparently a court functionary charged with maintaining etiquette and ceremony), and the *Laksamana*, or admiral (the title apparently being derived from a name in the *Ramayana*).[27]

The microcosm was completed by the sixteen *mentris* of the third rank and thirty-two officials of the lowest rank who were not permitted to bear the title of *mentri*, though the precise titles and functions of the offices are unknown. Winstedt points out that all *mentris* probably had some judicial duties in addition to their executive and administrative tasks,[28] but so little factual information is available that further conjecture would be hazardous.

24. *Ibid.*, pp. 72–73. Additional evidence that the *Bendahara* was most senior of the four ministers of the first rank is provided by Wilkinson, who points out that in state functions he was second in order of precedence to the Sultan. See R. J. Wilkinson, "The Malacca Sultanate," *Journal of the Malayan Branch of the Royal Asiatic Society*, XIII (Oct., 1935), 30. Note that an essay by the same author in 1912 bore the same title though the contents are different. See n. 8, above.

25. *Ibid.*, pp. 73–74; and Gullick, p. 8.

26. Winstedt, *Malaya and Its History*, p. 36. Although the Malacca port regulations have been lost, the Kedah regulations, which are probably similar, are extant. See Sir Richard O. Winstedt, "Kedah Laws," *Journal of the Malayan Branch of the Royal Asiatic Society*, VI (June, 1928), 2–7.

27. The duties of the *Laksamana* are suggested somewhat vaguely in the *Malay Annals*. See esp. pp. 106, 200–202 (Leyden translation). He seemed primarily to have been in charge of the Sultan's naval vessels and at the same time must have been charged with some menial duties at court.

28. *The Malays: A Cultural History*, p. 75.

Religion and magic were everywhere prevalent in the traditional Malay political system. The person of the Sultan, as well as his royal regalia, was sacred and inviolable, while representatives of the Sultan filling official positions in the state were also recipients of authority drawing from their association with the Sultan.[29] In addition, the entire structure of government was based on the macrocosmic-microcosmic conception of the universe with its cosmological ordering, a subject to which further attention will be directed later.

(4) Sources of Authority

Sources of authority to legitimatize political acts in pre-European Malaya might be divided into several interrelated categories. Most apparent is what social scientists, following the lead of Max Weber, have come to call "traditional authority." Political action is legitimate when it conforms to well-established and accepted practice and when it is carried out by a person who is designated for this role by rules also handed down from the past.[30] "Dead we lie wrapped by earth; alive we are wrapped by custom," as it was phrased in a Malay proverb.[31] While the authority of the Sultan and his court came to draw heavily from Islam, the institution of the ruler actually represents a segment of an earlier traditional political system that adopted the alien religion, possibly as a means of reinforcing the authority of the already existent rulers.[32] Moreover, as the Sultanate continued throughout time the fact

29. Skeat, pp. 36–37. The author further points out that this aura of divinity also encompassed the early European District Officer, who was regarded by rural Malays as an authorized representative of the Sultan. Crop failures and other natural disasters were regarded as instruments of divine will exercised by the supernatural DO.

30. See Max Weber (trans. by A. M. Henderson and Talcott Parsons), *The Theory of Social and Economic Action* (Glencoe, Ill.: The Free Press, 1947), pp. 341–45. According to Weber, political action is " 'traditional' if legitimacy is claimed for it and believed in on the basis of the sanctity of the order and the attendant powers of control as they have been handed down from the past. . . . The person or persons exercising authority are designated according to traditionally transmitted rules" (p. 341).

31. Quoted in Winstedt, *Malaya and Its History*, p. 33.

32. On the origins of Islam in Malaya, see Sir Richard O. Winstedt, "The Advent of Muhammadanism in the Malay Peninsula and Archipelago," *Journal of the Straits Branch of the Royal Asiatic Society*, No. 77 (Dec., 1917), pp. 171–75.

that it existed reinforced the belief that it should exist, and thus
custom went hand-in-hand with religion to provide the authority
for legitimatizing political decisions.

Not only did the Sultan derive authority from custom and religion, but he could also turn to a macrocosm-microcosm concept
of the universe in which the institution of the Sultan in the capital
city constituted a central point. The belief in the miniature universe on earth permeates traditional Malay thought and is also
common among the native tribes of Borneo.[33] The cosmological
ordering of the four ranks of officers who served the Sultan is
itself an attempt to duplicate the structure of the cosmos, and
only when earthly order mirrored the order of the Malay universe
would prosperity and happiness prevail on earth.[34]

According to the cosmological theories of Hinduism and Buddhism in Southeast Asia, which Heine-Geldern suggests were at
least partly adopted by the Muslim political systems of Malaya,[35]
Mount Meru constituted the hub of the universe, while the four
continents surrounded the mountain, one in each of the four
cardinal directions. On the slopes of Mount Meru lived the four
kings who were guardians of the earthly world, and the summit
of the mountain was the home of Indra, the Vedic war god, together with a constellation of lesser gods. The capital cities of

33. Sir Richard O. Winstedt, "Notes on Malay Magic," *Journal of the Malayan
Branch of the Royal Asiatic Society,* III (Dec., 1925), 16, describes a Dyak
legend in which a medicine woman fed an army with rice cooked in a chestnut-
sized pot and meat from a cauldron the size of a bird's egg. As Winstedt points
out, this magic feat was based on the Dyak belief in the miniature universe.

34. Heine-Geldern, pp. 1-2. As Heine-Geldern also points out, this emphasis
on earthly duplication of the universal order was a characteristic of the major
religions of South and East Asia (*ibid.,* p. 2), but it should be noted that there
were some important differences in the manifestations of these beliefs. For Lao
Tse, the good man was the man who knew the *Tao*—the man who ordered his
life in such a way that he was in perfect harmony with universal order. Thus, by
doing nothing one could accomplish everything. Similar philosophies, with numerous variations, of course, were to be found in Hinduism, Buddhism, and Con-
fucianism (see F. S. C. Northrop, *The Meeting of East and West* [New York:
The Macmillan Co., 1946], chap. ix). The primary difference between the cosmological concepts of these religions and the beliefs found in Malaya seems to
center more on means than on ends. In the major Chinese religions, for example,
the emphasis was placed almost entirely on the adjustment of individual attitudes to bring about this microcosmic duplication; in Malaya, primary importance was placed on ritual and on the need to simulate the forms of the universe; little attention was given to man's need to reshape his inward self through
introspection and contemplation.

35. *Ibid.* Except where otherwise noted, the following several paragraphs have
been drawn primarily from this valuable study.

the Southeast Asian states, influenced by this Indian tradition, then attempted to re-create this universe, either by planning the city architecturally around an actual mountain or—in later years —by providing a symbolic Mount Meru in the form of a temple. The ruler then became the microcosmic representative of Indra, or sometimes the reincarnation of Siva,[36] while his deputies represented the lesser kings and gods who resided on Mount Meru. The capital was thus the center of the empire just as Mount Meru was the center of the universe, and, symbolically, at the center of the capital stood the ruler, who derived his right to rule as well as the authority for his decisions from his position in the earthly microcosm.

The precise extent to which Muslim political systems were influenced by these Hindu beliefs is difficult to conclude with certainty. A number of traditions that have survived to present time in dress and rituals suggest considerable accretions from Hindu tradition, but the evidence is largely circumstantial. Moreover, the system of legal sanctions expounded in the *Malacca Laws* (*ca.* 1523) and the *Pahang Digest* (1596) combine Hindu and Muslim legal practices,[37] which seems strongly to imply that these Hindu political beliefs probably had a profound and continuing influence on the Muslim states.

Whatever the sources of the law, it is nevertheless clear that the legal codes served to implement the customary, religious, and magic authority of the rulers. At the level of the royal ruling class, the law provided a means of maintaining order, guaranteeing the privileges of the ruling class, and protecting the legitimacy of the Sultan. At the village level it is more difficult to generalize about law since it was really custom and therefore varied from village to village. The village headman was responsible for applying this custom, though it was usually necessary that his interpretations should fall within the area of village consensus, and the sanctions applied by the village were largely social.[38]

36. Siva is an ambivalent character in Hindu mythology second in importance only to Vishnu. In one of his faces, Siva was thought to be the patron deity of ascetics. It seems significant here that, according to Basham, p. 307, "on the high slopes of the Himalayan Mount Kailasa Siva . . . sits on a tiger skin, deep in meditation, and through his meditation the world is maintained."
37. Winstedt, *The Malays: A Cultural History*, pp. 99–118.
38. Gullick, pp. 116–17.

II. The Plural Nature of Malayan Society

(1) *Communal*

At the time of the 1957 census, in a total population of 6,278,763, Malaysians constituted 49.8 per cent of the total population of the Peninsula; Chinese, 37.2 per cent; Indians, 11.1 per cent; and others, 1.9 per cent.[39] Although the poor quality of migration statistics and the confusion of the war years have made analyses of past demographic trends hazardous,[40] it would seem that population growth in Malaya has now become fairly stabilized at a steady but high rate. The following tables summarize the growth of populations in the past and project these statistics into the future.

Table 1. *Malaya: Communal Composition, 1921–57* *

Community	Population in Thousands				Percentages			
	1921	*1931*	*1947*	*1957*	*1921*	*1931*	*1947*	*1957*
Total	2,907	3,788	4,908	6,279	100.0	100.0	100.0	100.0
Malaysian	1,569	1,864	2,428	3,127	54.0	49.2	49.5	49.8
Chinese	856	1,285	1,884	2,333	29.4	33.9	38.4	37.1
Indian	439	571	531	707	15.1	15.1	10.8	11.3
Others	43	68	65	112	1.5	1.8	1.3	1.8

* *Source:* Federation of Malaya, Department of Statistics, *1957 Population Census, Report No. 14* (Kuala Lumpur: Department of Statistics Press, 1960), Table 1.3, p. 3, with corrections based on more recent releases.

39. Federation of Malaya, Department of Statistics, *1957 Population Census, Report No. 1* (Kuala Lumpur: Department of Statistics Press, 1958), Table 1, p. 1. "Malaysian" was employed in the census of 1957 to include Malays, immigrants from Indonesia, and aborigines. Pakistanis and Ceylonese were tabulated under the category "others" in early reports, though they were apparently shifted to the category "Indians" in some of the later reports. The British in Malaya, interrupted by the interregnum of the Japanese occupation, departed from the international practice of gathering census material at the end of each even decade. The 1947 census was the first census after 1931, and the practice was followed in taking a census a decade later in 1957. It will be interesting to note the date of the next census in view of the forthcoming Malaysia scheme since the Bornean territories returned to the international census schedule in 1960 after also having conducted a census in 1947.

40. For a table summarizing probable migration between 1931 and 1953,

Table 2. *Malaya: Population Projections, by Community, 1957–82* *

		1957	1962	1967	1972	1977	1982
Total	Number (1000)	6,279	7,463	8,831	10,450	12,404	14,703
	Percentage	100.0	100.0	100.0	100.0	100.0	100.0
Malaysian	Number (1000)	3,127	3,709	4,381	5,168	6,081	7,130
	Percentage	49.8	49.7	49.6	49.5	49.0	48.5
Chinese	Number (1000)	2,333	2,771	3,282	3,888	4,616	5,502
	Percentage	37.1	37.1	37.1	37.1	37.2	37.4
Indian	Number (1000)	707	843	1,014	1,230	1,510	1,851
	Percentage	11.3	11.3	11.5	11.8	12.2	12.6
Others	Number (1000)	112	140	154	164	197	220
	Percentage	1.8	1.9	1.8	1.6	1.6	1.5

* This table has been adapted from *1957 Population Census, Report No. 14*, Table 7.13, p. 44.

It may be seen from these statistics that all communities are growing rapidly and that if this balanced rate continues the communal composition of the population in 1982 will not vary greatly from the present structure. Of course, these projections are based on medium fertility rates for each community, and if high or low rates should prevail in one or more cases the picture could look considerably different by 1982.[41]

In the geographic distribution of the major communal groups certain generalizations are possible, though, as later tables will show, the exceptions to these generalizations are numerous. The Chinese to a large extent are concentrated in a belt running from the southern tip of the Peninsula northwestwardly, with the concentration growing less dense on the inland side of the belt, and within this belt the highest concentrations are to be found in or around the larger towns. Malays, on the other hand, tend to be more evenly distributed throughout the Peninsula since the majority are rural dwellers. However, the following table demon-

---

which the authors point out cannot be accepted as entirely reliable, see Norton Ginsburg and Chester F. Roberts, *Malaya* (Seattle: University of Washington Press, 1958), p. 65.

41. For projections based on both high and low rates, see *1957 Population Census, Report No. 14*, Table 7.13, p. 44.

strates that all communities are to be found in sizable numbers in almost all geographic areas.

Table 3. *Malaya: Geographic Distribution of Population, by Community, 1957* *

	Total (1000)	Malaysian (1000)	Chinese (1000)	Indian (1000)	Other (1000)
Johore	927.6	444.9	392.4	71.0	19.2
Kedah	701.6	475.7	143.8	67.0	15.0
Kelantan	505.6	463.3	28.8	5.6	7.8
Malacca	291.2	143.2	120.7	23.2	4.0
Negri Sembilan	364.3	151.4	149.9	54.4	8.6
Pahang	312.9	179.1	108.1	21.8	3.9
Penang	572.1	165.0	327.3	69.0	10.7
Perak	1,221.4	484.9	539.4	178.5	18.7
Perlis	90.9	71.3	15.8	1.5	2.3
Selangor	1,012.9	291.4	488.6	201.0	31.8
Trengganu	278.2	256.3	18.1	2.7	1.0

* *Source: 1957 Population Census, Report No. 1, Table 1, pp. 1–3.*

That the Chinese tend to live in the urban centers while the Malays are distributed throughout the countryside may be observed in the following two tables and in the fact that of the eight cities of the Peninsula exceeding 50,000 population the Chinese are in the majority in all.[42]

Table 4. *Malaya: Communal Composition of Urban Population, 1947–57, by Percentages* *

	Malaysian		Chinese		Indian	
	1947	1957	1947	1957	1947	1957
1,000 population and over	21.1	22.6	62.3	63.9	13.8	10.7
10,000 population and over	19.0	21.0	63.1	62.6	14.7	12.8

* *Source: 1957 Population Census, Report No. 14, Tables 2.8, 2.9, p. 10.*

42. See *1957 Population Census, Report No. 1*, pp. 36–61. The eight cities are Kuala Lumpur, Georgetown, Ipoh, Klang, Johore Bahru, Malacca, Alor Star, and Seramban.

Table 5. *Malaya: Percentage of Total Population of Each Community Living in Urban Centers, by State* *

	Malaysian		Chinese		Indian	
	Over 1000	Over 10,000	Over 1000	Over 10,000	Over 1000	Over 10,000
Federation	19.3	11.2	73.0	44.7	41.1	30.6
Johore	20.2	13.6	64.9	29.6	31.7	22.5
Kedah	11.2	6.3	61.8	34.5	26.4	17.6
Kelantan	19.9	7.8	66.9	39.9	43.0	22.0
Malacca	8.8	6.5	52.2	44.0	26.8	21.1
Negri Sembilan	14.0	5.8	51.6	28.0	27.3	16.6
Pahang	18.2	8.7	76.4	43.5	41.7	24.5
Penang	30.4	24.9	79.1	70.4	73.0	67.1
Perak	17.4	9.3	79.7	37.6	40.7	26.4
Perlis	5.3	—	25.4	—	50.4	—
Selangor	30.2	21.4	84.0	57.2	43.8	34.9
Trengganu	29.6	15.8	82.6	57.1	62.5	48.2

* *Source: 1957 Population Census, Report No. 14, Tables 2.11, 2.12, p. 11.*

Merely demonstrating the multi-racial nature of Malaya does not in itself reveal the plural nature of Malayan society, for it is theoretically possible that a society highly diverse in racial composition could nevertheless become homogeneous and integrated without extensive intermarriage. And, in fact, though the end is far off, this is the often expressed goal of the present Alliance government. But, for the present time, the plurality of Malayan society manifests itself in the language; in social, cultural, and religious patterns; and in the structure of the economic system. All of these forces in turn exert pressures on the bureaucracy, which also has a plural nature of its own.

(2) *Linguistic*

In general, Malay is the language of the Malays; the Chinese largely speak Hokkien, Hakka, Cantonese, and Teochiu, though

Mandarin is taught in most schools and increasingly serves as the *lingua franca* of the Chinese-educated community; and the Indians mostly speak Tamil, though about 20 per cent use Malayali, Telegu, and other languages.[43] Since independence in 1957 there has been a concentrated attempt to implement Malay as the national language, and in fact it is the official policy of the present government to complete this conversion by 1967. However, as the following table dealing with literacy rates reveals, the task seems almost herculean, at least on the basis of these 1957 statistics.

Table 6. *Literacy Rates, 10 Years of Age and Over, by Community and Language, 1957, in Percentages* *

(*I. All Persons*)	Malay	English	Any language
Malaysian	46	5	47
Chinese	3	11	53
Indian	5	16	57
Others	14	58	78
All communities	25	10	51
(*II. Males Only*)	Malay	English	Any language
Malaysian	64	7	65
Chinese	4	14	70
Indian	6	21	70
Others	15	62	85
All communities	33	13	68

* *Source: 1957 Population Census, Report No. 14,* Tables 9, 9(1), 9A(1), 9B(1), 9C(1), and 9D(1), pp. 92–96.

(3) *Religious*

Although religious statistics have not been collected in Malaya since the census of 1931, it is generally recognized that Malays are almost exclusively Muslim; [44] Chinese are Confucian-Buddhist;

43. For the specific percentages of each of these linguistic groups, see *1957 Population Census, Report No. 14,* Tables 3.3, 3.4, p. 14.
44. The legal definition of "Malay" includes as one aspect acceptance as a member of the Islamic community.

Indians reporting themselves as Indian are largely Hindu while those calling themselves Pakistanis are probably Muslims; and that Christianity is limited almost entirely to a small minority of the Chinese and Indian communities. It would probably be an exaggeration to say that these religions and their related social customs are mutually incompatible, though it is apparent that conflicting social practices make the process of integration considerably more difficult. Coupled with this, both as an effect as well as a cause, is the communications barrier that blocks the horizontal exchange of information across communal lines. As later chapters will show, this problem is not present in the upper echelons of the government—where politicians, administrators, and military leaders can draw on the common experience of an English language education and in English find a common medium of communication—but it does contribute to continued compartmentalization of the lower levels of state and society.

(4) Economic

The economy of Malaya is as plural as the society on which it is superimposed, though economic divisions do not always follow communal demarcations. There are in fact, according to T. H. Silcock, not one but three Malayan economies.[45] There is the subsistence economy of the peasants, the mercantile economy of Penang and Singapore (and here the latter cannot be excluded), and—internationally most important—the mining and plantation economy. Of these three, the peasant economy is the most unsatisfactory, and—though recent concerted drives by the independent government are considerably improving the situation—Silcock's generalization about pre-Merdeka conditions still has a discouraging ring of truth in it: "[It is] an economy of poverty and chronic debt, relieved only in years of exceptional prosperity, . . . and normally at levels not much above the

45. See his *The Economy of Malaya* (Singapore: Donald Moore, 1957), and his most recent study of the subject. "The Economy of Malaya," in Calvin B. Hoover, ed., *Economic Systems of the Commonwealth* (Durham, N.C.: Duke University Press, 1962), chap. viii. This section on the Malayan economy is derived chiefly from these two sources. (Dates of publication will be inserted in parentheses to avoid confusion in future citations.)

appalling poverty of most of Asia." [46] It is true that some of the rice, vegetables, and somewhat more of the fish produced in the peasant economy find their way to the markets of Malaya, but the simple fact is that the peasant economy is barely able to sustain itself without having much left over for commercial uses. Thus, the importation of foodstuffs becomes a necessity as well as a luxury, and it is not unusual for these to constitute about 30 per cent of Malaya's net imports. Only in recent years have Malay fishermen been induced to take ice to sea to preserve their catch, and in fact the practice has not yet been accepted on the East Coast despite the urging of the Fisheries Department. Rice, the major item of the diet consumed by all communities, has never been grown in sufficient quantities to meet domestic needs; about 35 per cent of the nation's requirements must be imported.

The mercantile economy of Penang and Singapore has suffered from a narrowing of the geographic area that it serves, but at the same time the volume of trade has continually climbed with only minor setbacks and with the major interruption of the Japanese occupation. [47] The major corporations and agency houses of Singapore are European owned, but Chinese capital and human resources constitute an essential part of the economy. As in the mercantile economy, the large rubber estates and tin mines of the peninsula are European owned or operated, but the small estates and tin mines are still in the hands of Malayans, most of whom are Chinese. [48]

This continued dependence upon land as a source of livelihood —both in cash crops and in subsistence agriculture—has focused

46. *The Economy of Malaya* (1957), p. 1. For comments on improvements in the subsistence economy after 1959, see "The Economy of Malaya" (1962), pp. 366–67.

47. *The Economy of Malaya* (1957), pp. 7–12. The election of the apparently left-wing People's Action Party of Lee Kuan Yew in 1959 created a temporary economic recession in Singapore, but the economy seems to have recovered quickly once it became apparent that Mr. Lee's government was not as radical as its campaign oratory had suggested. Penang still enjoys certain free trade privileges inherited from the days of the Straits Settlements, but neither Penang nor Port Swettenham (the site of the newly improved Klang River docks), separately or together, equals the entrepôt importance of Singapore.

48. See G. C. Allen and Audrey G. Donnithorne, *Western Enterprise in Indonesia and Malaya* (London: George Allen and Unwin, Ltd., 1957), pp. 150–51. Individual small-holdings of rubber (in contrast to estate production) are chiefly Malay owned. (Silcock, "The Economy of Malaya" [1962], p. 332.)

Table 7. *Malaya: Economically Active Population, by Community and Industry Divisions in Percentages* *

	Total	Malaysian	Chinese	Indian	Others
Agriculture, forestry, hunting, fishing	26.5	45.0	13.1	1.4	13.3
Estate agriculture	31.0	28.2	27.2	54.3	5.3
Mining and quarrying	2.7	1.0	5.2	2.2	2.6
Manufacturing	6.3	2.6	12.6	3.5	2.1
Building and construction	3.1	2.2	4.2	3.9	2.6
Electricity, gas, and water	0.5	0.4	0.4	1.3	1.1
Commerce	9.0	3.1	16.5	10.4	5.9
Transportation, storage, and communications	3.5	2.6	3.8	5.1	4.6
Services	14.8	12.5	14.2	15.4	60.5
Unspecified or inadequately defined	0.8	0.6	1.2	0.8	0.7
Looking for work	1.8	1.9	1.7	1.8	1.2

* Source: This table was compiled by the author from information contained in *1957 Population Census, Report No. 14,* Table 12, pp. 111–22. All percentages have been rounded off to the first decimal place. The economically active population for each category is: Total, 2,164,861; Malaysian—1,023,729; Chinese—771,963; Indian—312,956; and others—56,213.

increased attention upon Malaya's land problems and has presented the administrative bureaucracy with a series of problems requiring prompt solutions. The bureaucracy has been hampered in the past by the fact that the subject of land is contained on the state list of the constitution and is thus not within the proper domain of the Federal Government. Yet, few of the states exhibited the imagination and determination to solve their own land problems, and, in addition, in many areas of Malaya the continuing Emergency forced land administration to be reduced to a very low priority. As a result, a commission in 1958 discovered that 116,000 applications for titles were awaiting decisions, 37,000 titles were awaiting registration, and 50,000 registered titles were awaiting issue.[49] By 1961 it was reported unofficially that this first figure had probably risen to about 140,000, but it is probable that

49. Federation of Malaya, *Report of the Land Administration Commission* (Kuala Lumpur: Government Press, 1958), p. 29.

the more recent decisions by the Federal Government to assume the leadership of land settlement schemes has by now considerably reduced this backlog.[50]

The fragmentation of land is another problem that has caused concern in Malayan land administration, and again much of it has been occasioned by Malayan social and religious customs. As a result of the Muslim laws of inheritance,[51] the Land Administration Commission in 1958 reported that, "without attempting to find fantastic cases," two examples might demonstrate fragmentation occasioned by social custom. In the first case, nine heirs owned a small plot in the following proportions:

$$\frac{12,522}{57,024}, \frac{12,552}{57,024}, \frac{6,276}{57,024}, \frac{3,080}{57,024}, \frac{1,540}{57,024}, \frac{1,464}{57,024}, \frac{732}{57,024}, \frac{1,569}{57,024}, \frac{10,893}{57,024}$$

In the second case, a plot of two and one-fourth acres, eight heirs shared the land in these proportions: [52]

$$\frac{1}{2}, \frac{1}{14}, \frac{1}{14}, \frac{1}{14}, \frac{1}{14}, \frac{331,737}{2,286,144}, \frac{27,909}{2,286,144}, \frac{130,242}{2,286,144}.$$

50. Although land is a state subject the Constitution contained one loophole that could permit the Federal Government to exert leadership if it chose to. Article 91(1) authorized the creation of a National Land Council made up of one representative from each state and an almost equal number of federal representatives. Under the provisions of the Constitution, resolutions approved by the National Land Council (presumably by a majority vote) are binding on all states and Parliament may then legislate in this area to execute these policies. The fact is that land administration has always been a subject of considerable interest to Kuala Lumpur, and the Federal Government inherited from the colonial government an administrative structure that could have considerable influence on land policies regardless of the legal provisions. In addition, the state governments, by acceptance of the district officer system and the posts of Commissioners of Lands and Mines, virtually recognized the hegemony of the Federal Government in matters dealing with land administration.

51. In brief, the Quran provides that "a male shall inherit twice as much as a female. If there be more than two girls, they shall have two-thirds of the inheritance; but if there be one only, she shall inherit the half. Parents shall inherit a sixth each, if the deceased have a child; but if he leave no children and his parents be his heirs, his mother shall have a sixth. . . . You shall inherit the half of your wives' estate if they die childless. If they leave children, a quarter of their estate shall be yours. . . . Your wives shall inherit one-quarter of your estate if you die childless. If you leave children, they shall inherit one-eighth. . . . If a man or a woman leave neither children nor parents and have a brother or a sister, they shall inherit one-sixth. If there be more, they shall equally share the third of the estate . . . without prejudice to the heirs" (4:11–12; this prose translation was taken from N. J. Dawood, *The Koran* [London: Penguin Books, 1956], pp. 355–56).

52. P. 63. *The Report* does not explain the missing $\frac{6,396}{57,024}$ in the first example.

Fragmentation of holdings in the peasant economy continues to be a problem, though the tendency now is for states to restrict the subdivision of land below certain economic limits by the provision that such titles cannot be registered and cannot be cited in court.[53] Thus, while legal fragmentation is diminishing, customary fragmentation may still be a problem.

The plural nature of Malayan society has produced one final anomaly affecting land administration that at least deserves mention. The nine Malay States of the Federation each has statutes setting aside Malay Reservations, and in these areas land can be alienated only to Malays and transferred only among Malays. Much of the land contained in Malay Reservations is area most suitable for the production of rice,[54] but in the past rural Malays have exhibited little enthusiasm for producing agricultural crops beyond their own immediate needs. To a limited extent, this has probably been circumvented in many cases where the Malay ownership of such land is more a façade behind which non-Malay financial interests own the produce of the land through Malay indebtedness, but it is not surprising that little statistical information is available on these practices.

III. The Origins and Effects of Social Heterogeneity

Whether it be in quotas for the Malayan Civil Service or in the practice of setting aside Malay Reservations, the lack of social and political homogeneity has had a profound effect on Malayan administration. Much of this lack of social consensus can be attributed simply to some of the basic religious and customary differences among the major communities, but to a great extent it also represents one of the less fortunate legacies of the colonial experience.

53. A leader in imposing this restriction was Kelantan, one of the most traditional of the Malay States, where the Land Code of 1938 restricted the fragmentation of land to plots no smaller than one-fourth acre.
54. Silcock, *The Economy of Malaya* (1957), p. 31.

(1) *Colonial Policies and Communal Separatism*

Wherever the British have been as colonial powers the cliché "divide and rule" is almost certain to be used to describe the colonial administration. It should not be our purpose to provide an apology for imperialism, for the colonial era was a simple fact of Western history, a fact that colonial powers and former colonies alike must now live with. Similarly, to look behind every colonial policy for the cunning and sinister motive that really caused a given decision to be made can only be a fruitless search except on rare occasions. Most important, to presuppose a thesis such as "divide and rule," at least in the case of Malaya, seems to ascribe to British colonial policy considerably more rationality than a study of the relevant colonial documents reveals it to merit.

To be sure, the continuing orientation of Britain in the Malayan Peninsula was more in the direction of the Malays than toward the immigrant communities. Most of the British administrators spoke Malay, but few were trained in an Indian dialect, and proportionately fewer still were fluent in Chinese.[55] The British generally regarded themselves as the protectors of the Malays, and, at least prior to World War II, Malaya was regarded as the home of the Malays and only the temporary residence of the alien communities—a view that could be more easily defended at that time in view of the large volume of traffic of immigrants back and forth between Malaya and their native homes.

On the whole, the British movement into the Malayan Peninsula was a peaceful operation, with a necessary resort to force against the established government occurring on only one occasion.[56] In each of the native states British protection was based

55. According to tabulations derived from Straits Settlements and Federated Malay States, *The Malayan Civil List, 1940* (Singapore: Government Printing Office, 1940), 138 officers were qualified in Malay, 41 in one dialect of Chinese, and 31 in one Indian dialect. Based on a rough estimate of the population of the Peninsula in 1940, this would mean that there was about one Malay-speaking MCS officer to every 15,000 Malays, while the proportions for Indians and Chinese would be 1:19,000 and 1:40,000 respectively.

56. The single military expedition against a native government came as a result of the murder of the first British Resident of Perak, Mr. J. W. W. Birch. Birch, a former Colonial Secretary of the Straits Settlements, was probably one of the worst possible choices for the difficult initial residential assignment in Malaya. He spoke no Malay, having come to the Straits Settlements from Ceylon, and his

on treaties in which the Sultan participated in the signing as a formal equal of the British sovereign. Thus, from the signing of the Treaty of Pangkor in 1874 forward, the British looked upon themselves as the protectors of the Malays and the treaties establishing the residency system gave an aura of legal sanctity to this emotional bias.

While the British attitude toward the Malays was paternalistic and protective, their policies in regard to the Chinese were largely pragmatic, devised on an *ad hoc* basis to fit the immediate needs with surprisingly little apparent recognition of the long-term problems engendered. There were undoubtedly some contacts between China and Malaya as early as the sixth century A.D., and there were some three hundred Chinese living in Malacca at the beginning of the seventeenth century; however, it was not until the development of the tin and rubber industries under British colonial direction that the great Chinese immigration into Malaya took place. British colonial reports continually recognized the value of this alien labor force, and individual administrators were quick to concede the economic worth of the enterprising and hard-working Chinese. Yet, the British found it exceedingly difficult to deal with the Chinese on political matters, and to govern them directly through the established system proved virtually impossible, at least in the early days of the FMS and the UMS. As a result, the British found it expedient to acquiesce in what appeared to be the inevitable and attempt to govern the Chinese community indirectly through the local Chinese headman, or "Kapitan China," who commonly held his title by virtue of being the head of the most powerful secret society of the area.[57] Although the last Kapitan did not disappear until 1930, with the

---

attitude is best summarized in his own words: "It concerns us little what were the old customs of the country nor do I think they are worthy of any consideration." (Quoted in G. P. Dartford, *A Short History of Malaya* [London: Longmans, Green and Co., 1957], p. 131.) The second Resident, J. G. Davidson, was untried since he resigned almost immediately after accepting the post to return to the security of his Singapore law office. The third Resident, Sir Hugh Low, whose task by then was doubly difficult, was one of the ablest colonial administrators Malaya was to have. For the single major clash between the British and an established Malay government (which in many ways bore more resemblance to a comic opera than to a war) and for details of several minor encounters, see C. Northcote Parkinson, *British Intervention in Malaya, 1867–1877* (Singapore: University of Malaya Press, 1960), *passim*, esp. chaps. x–xi.

57. On secret societies in Malaya, see Leon Comber, *Chinese Secret Societies in Malaya* (Locust Valley, N.Y.: J. J. Augustin, 1959).

rapid increase of the Chinese population, the increasing violence
of contests for power among secret societies, and with the establishment of the Chinese Protectorate, the method of governing
the Chinese necessarily became more direct.[58] But, while becoming more direct, the British were never successful in communi-
cating with the Chinese to the extent that they could with the
Malays, and in the Peninsula the mood seemed to be one of fatal
acceptance of the wall that separated the Chinese from the British administration.[59]

(2) *The Retreat to Extremes: The Emergency*

The open rebellion that began in 1948, officially labeled the
"Emergency," represented both a logical culmination of historical
trends as well as a break with attitudes of the past. Extending
for twelve years, the Emergency resulted in the loss of 11,043 lives
and cost the victorious side M $1.7 billion.[60] The definitive history
of the Emergency has not yet been written,[61] though its outlines

58. On the last Kapitan, see Victor Purcell, *The Chinese in Southeast Asia*
(London: Oxford University Press, 1951), p. 314. For a careful analysis of statistical data demonstrating the growth of the Chinese community in Malaya and
Singapore, see Victor Purcell, *The Chinese in Malaya* (London: Oxford University
Press, 1948), Appendix III. For an elaboration of the argument that the trend
was from indirect to direct government of the Chinese, see *ibid.*, p. 143. The
Chinese Protectorate was created in 1877, but it was many years before it was
effective beyond Singapore. Moreover, the primary role of the Protectorate was to
protect the Chinese from abuses by other Chinese and to suppress undesirable
(though usually profitable) practices within the community. See Ng Sien Yoong,
"The Chinese Protectorate in Singapore," *Journal of Southeast Asian History*, II
(March, 1961), 76–97.

59. Note that in 1938, in reply to questioning, it was revealed that the Secretary
of the Chinese Affairs Service—a pan-Malayan organization—spent 320 days per
year in Singapore, as contrasted with 22 in the FMS. (See Federated Malay
States, *Federal Council Proceedings* [Kuala Lumpur: Government Press, 1938],
p. B24.)

60. These figures are taken from the official estimates provided at the formal
close of the Emergency on July 31, 1960. See *Malay Mail* (Kuala Lumpur), July
30, 1960, p. 7. To avoid confusion, the symbol M $ will be used when the Malayan
dollar is intended ($1 = M $3).

61. The official historian of the Emergency has been named and the study
has been commissioned. However, there seems to have been some delay in the
production of the volume. There is a socio-political study of a sampling of the
communist terrorists (taken from among the defectors, or the "surrendered enemy
personnel"). See Lucian W. Pye, *Guerrilla Communism in Malaya* (Princeton:
Princeton University Press, 1956). There is a sketchy historical account written
by a British officer then serving on the staff of General Sir Gerald Templer. See

are clear enough to permit some relevant generalizations sufficient so far as the present study is concerned.

The origins of the Emergency are probably to be found as much in the history of Sino-British relations in Malaya as they are in the international communist movement. There can be little doubt that the Malayan terrorists were communist led and communist trained, but it is also obvious that they were almost entirely Chinese in composition. It would be a strange trick of history if only the Chinese should by nature be susceptible to the appeals of communism; thus it seems most likely that communism had its greatest appeal among the Chinese community for particular historical reasons. British colonial policy itself perhaps provides at least several of the more pertinent of these. The Emergency may have been part of a much larger international communist movement, but it seems probable that in Malaya any international conspiracy must have been furthered by the presence of a large unassimilated communal group of immigrant origin that felt itself estranged from the political and social order of the Peninsula. British colonial policy, probably more by accident than by design, contributed to some extent to this continuing attitude of separation.

The Chinese remained a colony almost to themselves for negative as well as for positive reasons. The Chinese seem to have a natural predilection for establishing district, provincial, clan, and secret society organizations, both in China and wherever they may migrate, and the British seemed content to let them do this because they had no ready alternative and because it was simply the most economical way to get the benefit of Chinese labor with

---

J. B. Perry Robinson, *Transformation in Malaya* (London: Secker and Warburg, 1956). A novel published in 1953 was described by Templer as an "authentic" description of the fighting in the jungles, but it suffers seriously from the superficiality of the author's understanding of the real problems faced among the Malayan Chinese. See Arthur Campbell, *Jungle Green* (Boston: Little, Brown, and Co., 1953). Erring to the other extreme, the foremost authority on the Chinese in Malaya replied to these views in a volume that is useful for research purposes despite the unfortunate presence of considerable unscholarly diatribes directed against Templer. See Victor Purcell, *Malaya: Communist or Free?* (Stanford: Stanford University Press, 1954). Several recent novels have taken some aspect of the Emergency as a theme, but in general the treatment thus far has been more romantic or sensational than sympathetic and understanding. Some useful information on the Emergency is contained in J. H. Brimmell, *Communism in South East Asia* (London: Oxford University Press, 1959).

a minimum of official expenditure. Thus, a newly arrived immigrant generally turned to his own association because it was the natural thing to do and because there was nowhere else to turn anyway. The Malayan Communist Party, which was formally established in Singapore in 1930, drew to its ranks the more sophisticated but equally unassimilated Chinese in much the same way as other organizations had been doing throughout the Peninsula for the preceding half-century. Yet, while it aspired to be pan-communal, it is nevertheless an historical fact that it attracted to the fold a coterie of followers almost exclusively Chinese.

For the Malays of the *kampongs* the ties of religion and tradition were sufficiently strong as to make the conversion to an ideology so sophisticated and alien to their simple life almost beyond the ability of most even to imagine.[62] Moreover, there was little attempt to propagandize communism as a means of improving the economic plight of the *kampong* dwellers, for it seems to be one of the most fundamental characteristics of the nature of rural Malay life that traditional subsistence and dependence only on what is immediately available constitute by far the best possible existence.

To the small group of the Western-educated Malay elite, that small percentage of the total Malay population that have moved from traditional villages into the urban centers, communism was equally unattractive, though for somewhat different reasons. That the ties of tradition were considerably weaker is evidenced by the mere fact that these Malays had left their native environment, though of course there were strong and continuing ties with the traditional way of life. However, most of these Malays, having received free primary and secondary education and often in later years having been the recipients of university scholarships, returned from their subsidized training to the employment of the government. Government employment in colonial Malaya was lucrative, prestigious, and provided at a higher level the same type of security that was to be found in the more traditional

62. I am heavily indebted to Pye, *Guerrilla Communism in Malaya*, pp. 49–51, 55–57, for many of the ideas presented in this section.

Malay life. For the educated urbanized Malay, as well as for his relatively untouched brethren in the *kampongs,* communism could only offer a social order inferior to the one he was already enjoying. Moreover, the British exhibited marked antipathy toward communist elements in Malaya, and the Malays, especially those of the English-educated class, regarded the British not as political adversaries but as paternalistic protectors of the Malay way of life.

Like the Chinese, the Indians too were an immigrant community who arrived in Malaya largely as a result of the opening of the country in the nineteenth and twentieth centuries. Unlike the Chinese, as Pye points out, they arrived with a much more positive orientation toward government. The very fact that both India and Malaya were under British domination made it possible to achieve a high degree of co-operation between the two governments. Numerous safeguards imposed by the British at both ends of the labor supply line considerably cushioned the initial shock of migration and largely removed the new immigrants from the danger of falling into the hands of the many unscrupulous exploiters who awaited them. The government both supervised the transportation of laborers and administered the Indian Immigration Fund, a fund begun by the FMS but supported primarily by the contributions of employers of Indian laborers that paid for transportation and provided medical care during and immediately after the voyage.[63] Newly arrived Chinese immigrants usually turned to their fraternal, clan, or secret societies for identification, and it was in this environment that the new process of political socialization took place. In contrast to this, Indian laborers had only to look to a paternalistic government for assistance, advice, or for a redress of any grievances.

The Emergency also owes a considerable debt to World War II, for it was at this time that an otherwise inchoate nationalist and communist movement was transformed into a disciplined

63. A summary of the history and the operation of the Indian Immigration Fund is contained in Aylmer C. Pearson, *Report on the Working of Various Departments of the Federated Malay States Government and on the Philippine Forest Bureau* (London: W. Straker, Ltd., 1914), pp. 3–11. (Pearson had been sent to Malaya and the Philippines to study administrative reforms that might be introduced into Borneo.)

military organization. Operating behind the Japanese lines, the predominantly Chinese MPAJA (Malayan Peoples Anti-Japanese Army) and the non-combatant support organization MPAJU (Malayan Peoples Anti-Japanese Union) may or may not have been effective against the Japanese,[64] but in the eyes of the Chinese they were the symbol of resistance while the Malays and the Indians were often regarded by the Chinese community as collaborators.[65] The British handling of the ill-fated Malayan Union scheme must also bear some responsibility for further alienating the Chinese community prior to the Emergency at the same time that it provided the catalyst that contributed to the first surge of Malay nationalism in the Peninsula.[66]

64. Pye, p. 69, questions the effectiveness of the guerrilla forces, but concludes that it is a credit to their "skill in propaganda that the MCP [Malayan Communist Party] was able to make so many believe so much with so little to go on." Two accounts of life with these communist-led forces support this thesis. See F. Spencer Chapman, *The Jungle is Neutral* (London: Chatto and Windus, 1950), and Dennis Holman, *Noone of the Ulu* (London: William Heinemann Ltd., 1958). Though it is not part of the purpose of either book to appraise the worth of these forces in the resistance movement, the reader is likely to put these books down with the distinct impression that most of the time of the guerrillas was taken up merely in trying to live in the jungles and very little time was devoted actually to attacking the Japanese.

65. Very little information is publicly available on the conduct of Malayans under the Japanese occupation. It is said unofficially that detailed reports were prepared on the associations and work of individual public servants, but, if they do in fact exist, they have not been made available. Some general statements may be found in Supreme Allied Command South East Asia, *Report on the British Military Administration of Malaya* (Kuala Lumpur: Government Press, 1946), Appendix XII. This document also mentions a confidential report prepared on the conduct of the Malay royalty, but this material is not available. Some hint of the findings may be seen in Great Britain, Colonial Office, Sir Harold MacMichael, *Report on a Mission to Malaya* (London: HMSO, 1946), p. 2.

66. The complicated politics of the Malayan Union plan have never received the scholarly attention deserved. Based on published accounts, on personal contacts, and on the personal correspondence of Sir George Maxwell for the period (which was opened to the author by the courtesy of the Secretary of the British Association of Malaya, London), the following tentative account can at least be pieced together.

The unification of Malaya, announced as the Malayan Union scheme by the Labour Government on October 10, 1945, was not a new departure in Malayan colonial policy. In 1932 a Colonial Office official, Sir Samuel Wilson, came to Malaya with a proposal for administrative reorganization similar in broad outline to the later Malayan Union proposals. The 1932 scheme was defeated by the opposition of the Malay rulers, a fact not lost on Wilson's young assistant, Edward Gent, by 1942 a high official in the Colonial Office. With Sir Edward directly responsible for the department concerned with colonial territories in Southeast Asia, the 1932 scheme was removed from the files for a second look. A Malayan Planning Unit was created in London to plan for the rehabilitation of Malaya, but the officials available to staff the group were largely younger men with little first-hand experience in Malaya, since most of the senior officers were in Japanese

Whether the open rebellion begun by the former resistance

hands. It was the attitude of the MPU that the reorganization proposals should be pushed through as quickly as possible after the war before the inevitable opposition of the rulers defeated the plan, as had happened in 1932.

The Malayan Union would have created a common citizenship for all communities and would virtually have erased state boundaries within the Union. The MacMichael mission (see n. 65, above) was carried out for the purpose of gaining the approval of each Sultan for the implementation of the Union. MacMichael was successful, but the tactics he employed were later to be questioned. His powers were twofold: he was to look into reports on the Sultans' conduct with a view toward advising the British Government on the desirability of retaining or deposing each of the Rulers, and he was also to seek each Ruler's signature on the treaties he had brought along, which were to be used as enabling acts leading to the creation of the Union. Supporters of the Malayan Union scheme argued that these simultaneous powers, though perhaps unfortunately juxtaposed, were not used by MacMichael to exert undue pressure, a position consistently maintained by MacMichael himself. However, a copy of an undated letter addressed to Sir George Maxwell from the Sultan of Kedah disputes this contention: "I was presented with a verbal ultimatum with a time limit, and in the event of my refusing to sign the new agreement, which I call the Instrument of Surrender, a successor, who would sign it, would be appointed Sultan. Members of the State Council were also compelled to sign and . . . to advise me to sign it. I was told that the matter was personal and confidential and was not allowed to tell my people what had taken place." A carbon copy of a memo dated February 11, 1946, addressed to a third party from the Yang di-Pertuan Besar and the major chiefs of Negri Sembilan recounts essentially the same story.

The Union, created on April 1, 1946, was stillborn. (See Great Britain, *Rules and Orders, 1946*, Vol. I, No. 463, pp. 543–71. For other relevant documents see Great Britain, *Parliamentary Debates, 1945–46*, Vol. 414, cols. 255–56; *ibid., Malayan Union and Singapore: Statement of Policy on Future Constitution* [London: HMSO, 1946, Cmd. 6724], and *ibid., Malayan Union and Singapore: Summary of Proposed Constitutional Arrangements* [London: HMSO, 1946, Cmd. 6749].) Opposition to the Union seems to have taken a curious route. The Sultan of Johore, the first signatory (whose co-operation was used as a lever on lesser Sultans), departed for London in March, 1946—several months after signing a MacMichael treaty—and in London he apparently called upon a retired MCS officer who was influential and highly respected. Earlier letters to the *Times* indicated the sympathy of the "old Malaya hands," and the Sultan apparently sought advice on how best to counter the Union proposals. (For earlier expressions of this sympathy in the *Times*, see Sir Richard O. Winstedt's letter of June 28, 1945 [p. 5], and the letters of Sir Frank Swettenham [October 29, 1945, p. 5 and November 6, 1945, p. 5].) Opinion was thereupon mobilized both in London and in Kuala Lumpur. In London it took the form of concerted and articulate support by the living notables of British colonial history, and a letter to the *Times* of April 16, 1946, reads like an index to a study of modern Malayan history. The letter was signed by Sir Cecil Clementi, Sir George Maxwell, Sir Frank Swettenham, and Sir Richard O. Winstedt, among others. Meanwhile in Kuala Lumpur, a Malay of royal birth from the household of the Sultan of Johore—and later to be *Mentri Besar* of that state—Dato Onn bin Jafa'ar, convened a Pan-Malayan Congress in March, 1946, and remained in close contact with the retired MCS officers in London through one of their number and with the Sultan of Johore. Evidence suggests that the former MCS officers also were not reluctant to intercede with friends in the Colonial Office on an informal basis, and that this might have played no small part in the reversal of the policy that was soon to follow. In Kuala Lumpur, the Pan-Malayan Congress became the United Malay National Organization, still under the leadership of Dato Onn.

Unfortunately, Chinese and Indian support for the Malayan Union plan was not forthcoming, thus strengthening the Malay criticism that equal citizenship was

forces in 1948 came at the direction of the international communist movement,[67] or whether it was "really only an accentuation
of the violence and lawlessness which was already sporadic," [68]
is a still unanswered question. It seems probable that it can best
be interpreted as stemming in part from the influence of the
communist-oriented MAPAJA leadership, in part as a reaction
against rising Malay nationalism, in part as delayed disillusion-
ment over the defeat of the short-lived Malayan Union; and in
part it represents the logical culmination of social and political
practices that prevented easy horizontal communications across
communal lines and virtually blocked communications between
the British administration and the Chinese masses in Malaya.

Whatever the causes of the Emergency, the results were the
hardening of communal lines and a legalization of physical and
social compartmentalization that had previously been based more
on convention than on law. While the Briggs Plan for the resettlement of Chinese rural communities into patrolled "New Villages"
was undoubtedly a military necessity, it also institutionalized the
separateness that had characterized the relationships of the two
major groups throughout Malayan colonial history. More important perhaps, it even further cut off the channels of commerce and
communication between Chinese and Malays, creating in fact a
Chinese peasant economy, an Indian peasant economy, and a
Malay peasant economy. According to Silcock:

---

being given to groups who felt no identification with Malaya. Comment in the
Chinese press in favor of the plan was unenthusiastic and was confined almost
exclusively to the communists. The Indian community was preoccupied with
events in the Indian Subcontinent and paid little attention to the creation or to
the demise of the Union until it was too late. (See Purcell, *The Chinese in Southeast Asia*, p. 390; Victor Purcell, "A Malayan Union: The Proposed Constitution,"
Pacific Affairs, XIX [March, 1946], 35–38; and Gerald Hawkins, "Reactions to the
Malayan Union," *Pacific Affairs*, XIX [Sept., 1946], 282–85.) Viewing the reactions of the Chinese and Indian presses it is difficult to refute the Malay charges
of the time that the immigrant communities were little concerned with politics in
Malaya.

67. The official view, supported by Pye, pp. 83–84, is that a general change of
policy was enunciated at the Asia Youth Conference in Calcutta in February,
1948, calling for an intensification of overt attacks on imperialist powers. This
decision was supposedly transmitted to the MCP by the Australian communist
Lawrence Sharkey. The original source of this information—also cited by Pye—is
Cecil H. Sharpley, *The Great Decision: The Autobiography of an Ex-Communist
Leader* (London: William Heinemann Ltd., 1952).

68. Purcell, *Malaya: Communist or Free?*, p. 61.

It can be reasonably argued that the enforcement of hurried resettlement of Chinese in Chinese villages, and regrouping of Indians in Indian settlements on estates, is the most permanently harmful result of the Communists' terrorism in Malaya. . . . It would inevitably have been difficult to instill any feelings of common interest into these rural people from such diverse cultures, but at least no major disintegrating forces were organized in the countryside. Terrorism has now set the stage for three separate lines of rural development instead of one. . . . A decade of such development on community lines could build barriers that might take a century to remove.[69]

While General Sir Gerald Templer felt it a military necessity to implement the Briggs Plan, which he did with great tactical success, he also undertook to introduce measures into Malayan government designed to demonstrate to the urbanized Chinese that they were to be given official status in the Peninsula. Part of this policy included opening the Malayan Civil Service to non-Malays, on a quota basis of four Malays to each non-Malay, a recruitment policy that has survived intact to the present time.[70]

(3) *The Legacy of the Emergency*

The Emergency has ended, but its lingering effects are still apparent. There is the continuing suspicion on the part of many in Malayan government that the communist forces were as much dissipated by economic and political factors inimical to their cause as they were defeated by a military campaign. It is probably true that many sympathizers to the communist cause who might have taken an active part in the fighting at one time simply gave up the battle and returned quietly to their homes to resume a normal life. In this sense, so the reasoning of some skeptics goes, the Emergency was more suspended than ended, and this suspension can achieve permanence only if responsible officials keep watchful eyes open until a more general consensus emerges that transcends communal boundaries.

The present Alliance Government, in office since 1955, is firmly committed to a policy of creating Malayans with political ties to

69. *The Economy of Malaya* (1957), pp. 7–8.
70. For a fuller discussion of these quotas, see chaps. v and vi below.

the Peninsula regardless of communal origins. But the task is a difficult one. The Prime Minister and Cabinet must always walk a tightrope between the outer fringes of the Malayan Chinese Association, where there is always the threat of a defection toward the left, and the more conservative elements of UMNO, which cannot fail to be attracted by the Malay-supremacy policies of groups such as the Pan-Malayan Islamic Party. Current drives for linguistic unity through the universal adoption of Malay in the Federation have strong appeal to the Malays, but it is always a difficult job of salesmanship to make such a program attractive to the non-Malay communities. The government has had to stand firmly behind the language proposals, but at the same time dispel the suspicions of non-Malays that this represents another manifestation of alleged Malay supremacy. Thus far, the present government has done an excellent job of blazing a narrow trail through the communal thickets, and, presuming the continuing vitality of the regime, perhaps these paths can be broadened in time, and thus provide security against encroachment by the underbrush during periods of less favorable economic and political circumstances.[71]

Such then is the social, cultural and historical environment within which Malayan bureaucracy must function. The modern bureaucratic machine is superimposed on a society that is itself schizophrenic, a society that in some sectors is decidedly modern while in others it is much more characteristic of the traditional model. The society is thus plural not only in racial composition, but also in cultural characteristics. Primarily as an effect of these causes, the economic and political systems are similarly plural in nature. Like the mercantile economy, the plantation economy, and the political institutions of government, the bureaucratic superstructure was a direct outgrowth of the Malayan colonial experience, and the origins of this bureaucratic machine must therefore be considered in some detail.

71. Since it is the official policy of the government that communalism is not to become a major political issue, the researcher in Malaya has considerable difficulty in gathering communal statistics. In fact, even where such official information has been collected, the government is extremely reluctant to release it. Similar problems occur in India when the researcher attempts to collect caste data.

2

Colonial Bureaucracy and the
Malayan Colonial Experience

In the colonial period, as in the days prior to the penetration of European influence, the shape of Malayan administration was influenced largely by events in the Indian Subcontinent. Although previously these imported institutions and practices had originated among the Hindus, on this latter occasion India represented only a brief stopover on the road from England to Malaya. Yet Indian experience influenced the character of Malayan bureaucracy even from the beginning of the British period, and, in those early days, the instrument by which these experiences reached the Peninsula was the English East India Company.

I. Malayan Bureaucracy under Company Rule

(1) *The English East India Company*

The London East India Company, the lineal ancestor of the English East India Company, was created by authority of a royal charter granted by Queen Elizabeth I on December 30, 1600. Slightly more than one year later the first fleet of East Indiamen set out for Southeast Asia in search of spices. Due in part to the pressures of international and domestic competition in the spice trade and in part to unfortunate political involvements at home, the original London Company foundered financially in 1693. King William III, in granting a charter to the newly formed East India

Company in 1698,[1] intended that it should assume the monopolistic privileges of the faltering London Company, but the latter, through adroit financial maneuvering, delayed its own demise until a compromise could be effected. The result of this compromise was the Charter of Union of 1708, which created the United Company of Merchants Trading to the East Indies, popularly termed almost throughout its history as the English East India Company.[2] Although the Company's interests were originally in the Southeast Asian area (in 1773 it actually established a trading factory at Balambangan, off the coast of North Borneo),[3] international rivalries eventually forced it to confine its early activities to the Indian Subcontinent, and further involvement in Southeast Asia was to be left to a later century.

The formal organization of the East India Company on the eve of its arrival in Malaya consisted in broad outline of a policy-making assembly, an executive arm, and a governmental review board. The legislative body was the General Court of Proprietors,[4] the executive arm was the less unwieldy Court of Directors,[5] and the supervising agency of the Crown was the Board of Commis-

1. The text of the Charter is reprinted in a number of secondary sources. The text consulted here, however, was a damaged quarto, held in the library of the University of Singapore, that was printed in London by an unnamed publisher in 1766.
    2. The popular title will be employed throughout this study. For the Charter of Union, see 9 Anne c. 7 (1708).
    3. The factory was sacked by the Sulus. See K. G. Tregonning, *Under Chartered Company Rule* (Singapore: University of Malaya Press, 1958), p. 17, n. 1.
    4. In the General Court, which was instructed by the Charter of 1698 to meet quarterly, voting was weighted according to the amount of stock owned, varying from one vote for a minimum of £1,000 of stock to four votes for stock in excess of £9,999. This paragraph draws heavily from a semiofficial compendium of Parliamentary Acts affecting the Company, compiled by the distinguished historian and Assistant-Secretary (later Secretary) to the Court of Directors. See Peter Auber, *An Analysis of the Constitution of the East-India Company* (London: Kingsbury, Parbury and Allen, 1826). Also see C. H. Philips, *The East India Company, 1784–1834* (Manchester: Manchester University Press, 1940).
    5. The Court of Directors was composed of twenty-four proprietors, each of whom was an English subject holding a minimum of £2,000 in Company stock. Although the Court of Directors was probably intended originally to serve as the executive committee, and this fiction continued throughout the life of the Company, in practice it achieved considerable independence from the larger General Court of Proprietors. It was in fact the Court of Directors that was competent to fill many of the lucrative foreign posts. Mention might also be made of the Secret Committee, a select group of not more than three Directors, charged on behalf of the Court of Directors with responsibility for business matters of a highly political nature, the dissemination of which might have been injurious to the Company's interests.

sioners for the Affairs of India.[6] Together, these institutions were responsible for appointing company servants to serve in the Indian presidencies, and thus also to possessions in the Straits of Malacca, which were ruled as appendages of the Subcontinent until 1867.

(2) *Origins of British Influence in Southeast Asia*

The lasting era of British influence began on a small island off the coast of Kedah in 1786, where the merchant-adventurer Francis Light, in rather ill-defined association with the East India Company, established a trading factory. The Company, although it belatedly conferred the title Superintendent of Trade on Light, initially exhibited little interest in Prince of Wales Island, at one point even refusing to honor the responsibilities implied—if not actually contained—in the instrument transferring possession of the island from the Sultan of Kedah to the Company.[7] However, even the businesslike Directors in London were unable to ignore the glowing accounts of the island's potential returned by Light and each of his next three successors on Penang, and in 1805 the small island was elevated to the status of an Indian Presidency on equal footing with the Bombay, Madras, and Bengal Presidencies of the Subcontinent.

6. The Board of Control, as it was popularly known, was established as a political compromise by the Regulating Act of 1784 (24 Geo. III c. 25). The Board was responsible for approving or disapproving all actions of the Court of Directors dealing with civil and military revenues in Company possessions. In addition, though it could not nominate candidates, the Board was required to pass on all nominees to vacancies in the Indian presidencies.

7. The official name of Penang was Prince of Wales Island, but the popular name continued to be employed except in some official correspondence. There is considerable difference of opinion among historians concerning the extent of the Company's commitment under the instrument of transfer negotiated and signed by Light. D. G. E. Hall, *A History of Southeast Asia* (London and New York: Macmillan and Co., 1958), pp. 434–36, argues convincingly that the agreement prepared and signed by the Company was so worded as to induce the Sultan to believe that he was to receive the Company's protection. In addition, Light had this understanding also and gave verbal assurances to the Sultan. However, the following year the Company refused to make a positive military commitment to the Sultan, whereupon Kedah attempted unsuccessfully to drive the British from the island. In 1821 the Siamese deposed the Sultan while the Company stood aside. Hall concludes that "from the point of view of strict legality the sultan was undoubtedly wrong, but there can be equally no doubt that in occupying Penang the Company assumed responsibility towards Kedah which it shamefully refused to recognize."

During its first half-decade as a Presidency, Penang was teeming with activity in an air of optimism and expectations, but the illusion of its inflated worth was soon to be shattered. By 1816 the Company was reminding the Presidency with increasing frequency that it was falling far short of its expectations, both economically and strategically.[8] As an economy measure Penang was united administratively with the former Dutch possession of Malacca and the newly established island base of Singapore in 1826,[9] and four years later this new administrative entity, the Straits Settlements, was reduced from its exalted status and again placed under the wing of the Bengal Presidency.

Colonial policies and institutions thus were eventually to radiate into the Peninsula from the three peripheral bases, Singapore, Malacca, and Penang, which together constituted the Straits Settlements. Moreover, the civil service that today staffs the non-elective posts of Malayan government is itself a direct descendant of the original Company civil service that was centered in the Straits Settlements. Many of the institutions, practices, and values that are to be found in the modern Malayan bureaucracy were imported to the Peninsula at this time, and thus this Company bureaucracy merits at least cursory attention.

(3) *The Company Service in the Malayan Area*

The term "civil service," according to Sir Edward Blunt,[10] was first used by the English East India Company to distinguish the

8. For example, see "Straits Settlements Records," Vol. C2, *Penang: Letters from London, 1815–1816,* dated February 7, 1816. Hereinafter this series will be abbreviated "SSR." The cataloguing system of the National Archives, Singapore, has been used throughout.

9. Malacca, having been wrested from the Portuguese by the Dutch in 1641 was administered by the British after the Napoleonic armies overran Holland. The settlement was returned to the Dutch temporarily in 1818 but reverted to the British pursuant to the Anglo-Dutch Treaty of 1824 delineating spheres of influence in Southeast Asia. Singapore was established by Thomas S. (later Sir Stamford) Raffles in 1819 against the wishes of the Company. Though the population probably did not exceed 150 at that time, Singapore by its ideal location and through Raffles' free-trade policies grew rapidly, and by the time of the Anglo-Dutch Treaty its importance had considerably outstripped that of Malacca. In recognition of this growing importance the administrative capital was moved from Penang to Singapore in 1832.

10. *The I.C.S.* (London: Faber and Faber, Ltd., 1937), pp. 1–2.

Company's civilian employees from those of the military, maritime, and ecclesiastical establishments. Though it is of course difficult to pinpoint the precise date that it entered the lexicon of bureaucracy, it seems to have been well enough established by the close of the eighteenth century to have appeared without elaboration in the Charter Act of 1793. The Company further distinguished two categories of civil servants, the covenanted and the uncovenanted. The former, containing the positions most sought after, entailed the posting of a bond of £500 as security for the Company against the breaking of the servant's oath to execute the duties of his post honestly and faithfully. Uncovenanted posts often were considerably less lucrative (though they might not have been had all covenanted servants adhered to the letter and the spirit of their oaths) and certainly less prestigious.

During the period of rule by the English East India Company civil servants posted to the Eastern Presidency did not carry with them an identifying title as was the practice in the Subcontinent, where the adjectives "Bengal," "Madras," or "Bombay" usually preceded the term "civil service." While the Charter of 1793 had practically trifurcated the Company service,[11] servants in the Straits area carried no distinctive title, for there was in fact no distinct service. Civil officers in the Straits area were generally detached from the Bengal civil service while military officers were usually seconded from the Madras establishment.[12] From time to time suggestions were to be heard that China might be a likely source of replacements in the Company's covenanted service, but the proposals always foundered because at the time the Straits area could not afford the additional expenses that such transfers would have entailed.[13]

11. On this point, see *ibid.*, p. 2. This trifurcation, probably unintended, was brought about by laying down the rule that vacancies in each Presidency could be filled only by officers serving in the Presidency where the vacancies occurred.
12. See Memorandum from the Governor General of India in Council to Lord Stanley, dated November 7, 1859, in Great Britain, House of Lords, *Parliamentary Papers*, XL (1862), 592.
13. For example, see *ibid.*, paragraph 9, and "SSR" Vol. S28, *Governor, Letters from India, 1860*, dated December 21, 1860, p. 264. It is fascinating to speculate about the historical course of British-Malayan relations had there been a sizable influx of Chinese-speaking, China-centered officers sufficient to temper the Malay-centered character of the Company service and later of the Colonial Service. Such speculation at this point is, however, purely academic. The basic problem was that

Recruitment to the service of the East India Company was at first exclusively by patronage to all ranks, though the practice had been proscribed in the case of the higher posts by the time of the creation of the Eastern Presidency on Penang.[14] While the Company took elaborate precautions to eliminate the most blatant examples of favoritism and nepotism, the practice of patronage continued in recruitment to lower posts in the Company's service.[15] The Company collectively always seemed suspicious of patronage as an institution, but the Directors individually found the practice too attractive to abandon completely.

During the period of rule by the English East India Company, wages—both in the Straits Settlements and in the Indian Subcontinent—were not commensurate with responsibilities. The Company had initially encouraged private trading as a means of supplementing the meager salaries, but it soon became apparent that losses in commerce far outstripped savings in the cost of maintaining the establishments. The Company then reversed its policies and proscribed all private trading, but such a drastic measure was highly ineffective since it had to be enforced through senior servants located far from London, who themselves stood to lose the most from the conscientious enforcement of the Company's edict. While private trading was probably to be found in the Straits area just as it was in India—and Malaya was certainly even farther removed from London—Company servants in Southeast Asia suffered the disadvantage of being posted to an area that was less attractive to the enterprising individualist than was India. Supplying few of the products popular in nineteenth-century Europe, the Company itself found it difficult to break

---

salaries were considerably more attractive in Hong Kong than in the Straits of Malacca, and it would have involved considerable expenditures to make the service competitive.

14. Patronage to the senior posts had been proscribed in the Charter Act of 1793.

15. Recruits to the Company's service were required to sign an affidavit affirming (1) that their appointment was gratuitously made, (2) that only the listed Directors were known personally, (3) that the person named was the intermediary who introduced the recruit to the Director recommending the appointment, and (4) that to the best of the recruit's knowledge "no person has received or is to receive any pecuniary consideration or anything convertible in any mode into pecuniary benefit" as a result of his appointment. An actual example of such an affidavit has been reprinted as Appendix A, below.

even in the Straits area, and thus it was virtually impossible for its servants to supplement their incomes greatly by private trading, whether it might have been accepted or illicit.

In retirement benefits, as in salaries, the Straits area was considerably less attractive than the Subcontinent. By 1826 Penang was the only Presidency not offering an annuity plan, and when the first plan was suggested by the Company in 1828 the requirement of twenty-five years service in the Straits Settlements made it appear probable that few officers would live to enjoy the fruits of their lifetime labors.[16] The resulting discontent of the servants in the Eastern Presidency caused the Company to drop the plan at the time, and it was to be almost at the demise of the Company before the servants in the Straits of Malacca were to enjoy retirement privileges similar to those of their colleagues in the Subcontinent. Similarly, home leaves came rarely in the Straits of Malacca, and when leave was taken it was an expensive undertaking from a point so far distant from England.[17]

After a brief flurry of optimism in the early nineteenth century, the Eastern Presidency offered few inducements to attract competent and energetic Company servants until Singapore was well established and had begun its process of phenomenal growth. Thomas S. (later Sir Stamford) Raffles was of course an exception, but it seems significant that between the era of Raffles (who left Singapore for the last time in 1823) and the Treaty of Federa-

16. A Mr. Anderson, speaking before the Council in Penang in 1828, commented that "averting to the well established fact of the insalubrity of this climate, and the alarming mortality amongst the Members of the Civil Service, it cannot be a matter of much surprise that a partial, if not a general feeling of depression and despondency exists. Most of us cherish an anxious desire to revisit our native country. Few indeed can reasonably anticipate this, if the period of servitude is prolonged to 25 years. . . ." See "SSR," Vol. A57, *Penang: Consultations, 1828,* pp. 121–22. The life expectancy indeed was not lengthy for civil servants in Penang and it seems probable that few would have lived to collect retirement benefits under this scheme. Of the 21 servants appointed to the Presidency in 1805, only 1 of the 16 who served their entire careers in the Straits Settlements was living in 1828 (23 years of service). Two servants had died with more than 20 years of service, 1 with 15 years, 4 with more than 10 years, 1 with 5 years, 6 with less than 5 years, and 1 died on the day he disembarked at Penang. See *ibid.,* pp. 124–25.

17. Although there was always a time lag between the implementation of benefits for civil servants in the Indian Presidencies and in the Eastern Presidency, it is remarkable that these benefits were available at all. Most of the benefits enjoyed by officers of the Malayan public services today have their roots in the early schemes of the Company Civil Service.

tion, a period of almost three-quarters of a century, Malayan administration was characterized by a succession of adequately competent but generally colorless civil servants, from whom there has been received remarkably little in the manner of memoirs and reminiscences, and about whom the literature and folklore are signally scarce.[18]

(4) *Demise of the Company*

The East India Company of the mid-nineteenth century had become a political anomaly, not uncharacteristic of so many British institutions of government. The Kumpani Bahadur, as it was popularly known in India, had emerged as a pragmatic answer to an unimagined administrative task. The Company was a joint-stock corporation, intended as a profit-making body, founded on the statement of Parliament that ". . . schemes of conquest . . . are measures repugnant . . . to the policy of this nation."[19] Yet by the time of the Indian Mutiny of 1857 John Company ruled an empire, albeit an empire that the Court of Directors had not always been eager to acquire and to enlarge.

Stewardship over such an empire was at first explicable as a necessary adjunct of the Company's original purpose of trade, but gradually the importance of commerce diminished as the role of governing increased. When the English East India Company lost its monopolistic privileges in 1833 and was retained in India chiefly for administrative purposes, the basic nature of the Company and its *raison d'être* were altered. Macaulay's speech before Commons on the retention of the Company recognized that

it is strange—very strange—that a . . . society of traders . . . should be entrusted with the sovereignty of a larger population . . . than are under the direct management of the Executive Government of the United Kingdom. But . . . that Empire is itself the strangest of all

18. Malaya eventually produced its share of scholarly and imaginative administrators in the best tradition of the ICS, but it was a long drought between Raffles, the relative moderns such as Clifford and Swettenham, and the contemporaries, such as Winstedt, Purcell, and Gullick.

19. This statement was contained in the Regulating Act (24 Geo. III c. 25 1784).

political anomalies. . . . The strangest of all Governments . . . is designed for the strangest of all Empires. . . .[20]

The "strangest of all governments" therefore continued to govern the Indian Empire until the Mutiny of 1857 caused it to collapse on its weakened foundations on September 1, 1858.[21] At this point the governance of the Straits Settlements also passed from the Company to the Crown, in form as well as in fact.

II. The Colonial Office Period of Malayan Administrative History

(1) *Transfer of the Straits Settlements to the Colonial Office*

Although the administration of India had been removed from the hands of a joint stock company, the position of the Straits Settlements still remained anomalous. Penang, Malacca, and Singapore continued to be regarded as appendages of India, and thus the hierarchy of authority ran from the Crown to the Straits Settlements by way of the India Office and Bengal. Due in part to the agitation of the Singapore merchants and in part to the sympathetic views of Lord Canning, then Governor-General of India, Parliament in 1866 enacted a "Bill to Provide for the Government of the 'Straits Settlements,'" which placed the control of administration in the hands of the Foreign Office and severed an attachment to India that had lasted for more than three-quarters of a century.[22]

20. Great Britain, *Hansard's Parliamentary Debates, 1833*, XIX, 515–16.
21. See Great Britain, *Sessional Papers, 1857–58*, II, 286, "A Bill for the Better Government of India."
22. The arguments of the merchants against the continued administration of the Straits Settlements through the India Office and Bengal were contained in a petition submitted to Parliament in 1862. (See Great Britain, *Sessional Papers, 1862*, XL, 583.) Briefly, it was argued that the needs and potentialities of the Straits Settlements had too often been seen from a strictly Indian point of view, that the judicial machinery had never kept pace with the rapid development of Singapore, and that Singapore was often regarded by the Indian government primarily as a penal colony for Indian felons. For an expression of the sympathetic concurrence of Lord Canning, see *ibid.*, p. 594. For the Act that severed the historic tie with India, see Great Britain, *Sessional Papers, 1866*, V, 327–30.

(2) Examination Tie with Other Colonial, Indian, and Home Services

The transfer of the Straits Settlements from the India Office to the Colonial Office did not have an immediately apparent effect on the character of Malayan administration. Responsibility for the selection of young men to fill Straits Cadetships devolved upon the Secretary of State for the Colonies and in 1869 a formal qualifying examination was introduced. However, even this did not follow the open competition of the ICS. Following the practice of the Ceylon Service (after 1855) and the Hongkong Service (after 1861), participation in the examination was limited to those previously nominated by the Colonial Secretary. This method of prior selection continued until the recruitment procedures of the ICS were adopted in 1882, and in 1896 the syllabi of examinations were standardized for the ICS, the Home Civil Service, and the Eastern Cadetships (which by this time included Ceylon, Hongkong, and Malaya).[23]

23. Except where otherwise noted, information dealing with the development of the public services from the administrative transfer of 1867 to 1919 is derived chiefly from Straits Settlements and Federated Malay States, Commission Appointed by His Excellency the Governor of the Straits Settlements and the High Commissioner of the Federated Malay States (Sir John A. S. Bucknill, Chairman), *Report* (London: HMSO, 1919). By the Treaty of Pangkor of 1874 Britain received permission for the stationing of a British officer in Perak and thus began the penetration inland from the Straits Settlements. Similar agreements followed with each of the Native States of the Peninsula, the last signatory being Johore in 1914. In 1896 four of these states (Perak, Selangor, Negri Sembilan, and Pahang), with British urging, united to become the Federated Malay States, a nominally independent British Protectorate. The remaining five states, individually under the wing of British protection (Perlis, Kedah, and Kelantan—after passing from Siamese suzerainty in 1909—Trengganu and Johore), became collectively known as the Unfederated Malay States. In fact, the relationship of Britain to the FMS and to the UMS differed more in degree than in kind—so much so that Sir George Maxwell in private correspondence referred several times to the "act of Federation" and the "act of Unfederation."

When the Straits Settlements was transferred in 1867 servants posted to each of the Settlements became colonial servants and ceased to be considered as seconded ICS officers. Appendix A of the Sterling Scheme of 1903, by designating certain posts as reserved for administrative cadets, contained the first suggestion of a "Straits Settlements Civil Service" (a title that seems to have come into currency only in 1920, however) and a "Malayan Civil Service." The latter term appeared occasionally and by the time of the Bucknill Commission *Report* of 1919 seems to have been accepted as a generic title for administrative officers of the Cadet Service serving in the Straits Settlements, the Federated Malay States, and the Unfederated Malay States.

For the Treaty of Pangkor of 1874, the beginning of the British Resident Sys-

On the basis of the open competition administered by the Civil Service Commission in London, applicants were given their choices of the three services according to their relative standings. The Bucknill Commission in 1919 reported that in general top-rated examinees with private resources usually chose the Home Service, while those without private incomes often opted for the ICS. The Eastern Cadetships were frequently left with the remaining examinees, who had no choice, and among these the order of preference was usually Ceylon, Hongkong, and finally Malaya.

(3) *Unification and Reorganization of the Colonial Services*

When Ceylon, Hongkong, and Malaya were combined into an Eastern Service it was anticipated that there would be considerable interchange of officers among the individual services, but the diversity of languages, the inconsistent classification of posts, and the highly dissimilar salary scales made such transfers unusual. Nevertheless, the fiction of a unified Eastern Service continued until it was absorbed into the greater, but almost equally fictitious, Colonial Administrative Service.

Created in 1932, the Colonial Administrative Service was the first stage of a general reorganization intended to unify all administrative, technical, and professional services throughout the colonies into a combined Colonial Service, but this, again, existed primarily on paper.[24] All officers of the Colonial Service sup-

---

tem of administration, and the Treaty of Federation of 1896, see Sir George Maxwell and William Sumner Gibson, eds., *Treaties and Engagements Affecting the Malay States and Borneo* (London: James Truscott and Son, Ltd., 1924), pp. 28–30; 70–71. On the Treaty of Federation also see Federated Malay States, *Correspondence Respecting the Federation of the Protected Malay States* (Taiping, Perak: Government Press, 1896). On the Sir George Maxwell correspondence, see chap. i, n. 66, above.

24. This unification of the many diverse services grew out of the *Report* of the Warren Fisher Committee of 1930, the provisions of which were introduced in stages beginning in 1932 by the Secretary of State for the Colonies after approval in principle by the Colonial Office Conference in June, 1930. Documentation on this reorganization is contained in Great Britain, *Sessional Papers, 1929–30,* Vol. VIII, "Report of a Committee on the System of Appointment in the Colonial Office and the Colonial Services" (Cmd. 3554); *ibid.,* Vol. IX, "Summary of Proceedings of the Colonial Office Conference, 1930" (Cmd. 3628); and *ibid.,* "Appendices to the Summary of Proceedings" (Cmd. 3629). For a sanguine

posedly could be transferred among the various colonies and protected states, but such transfers were infrequent, and even methods of recruitment varied considerably among the territories. Administrative officers were selected by the Colonial Office, but technical (and some professional) personnel were usually recruited directly by the colonies and protected states through the Crown Agents for the Colonies, and in these cases salaries, classifications of posts, and conditions of service varied so greatly that "unification" in fact meant very little.

Although the Warren Fisher Committee recommended the continuation of the competitive qualifying examination for entrance into the Eastern-Service component of the Colonial Administrative Service, the Colonial Office Conference was unwilling to accept dual procedures of recruitment to the Asian and African services. However, the Conference did accept the Committee's conclusion that in the case of Africa, for a variety of reasons, "it would be inexpedient . . . to rely on the test of written examination." [25] As a result, the competitive entrance examination for the Eastern Service was abolished, and the Malayan Civil Service was severed from its last historic tie with the ICS. Qualifying examinations administered at the close of the Colonial Administrative Course at Oxford or Cambridge at one time served much the same purpose as the entrance examination, but this practice was permanently disrupted by World War II. At the present time there is neither a competitive recruitment examination nor a rigid post-entry administrative course. Only the routine confirmation examination remains as a reminder of the system established in 1869.

In 1954, three years prior to the independence of Malaya, the term Colonial Service was dropped in favor of the less political title "Her Majesty's Overseas Civil Service." [26] Simultaneously, plans were made in Malaya and London for long- and short-range

account of unification by a member of the Colonial Office, and later Deputy Under-Secretary of State for the Colonies, see Charles Jeffries, *The Colonial Empire and Its Civil Service* (Cambridge: Cambridge University Press, 1938), chaps. v–vii.

25. Cmd. 3554, p. 20.
26. See Great Britain, Colonial Office, *Reorganization of the Colonial Service* (London: HMSO, 1954), pp. 6–7 (Colonial No. 306).

training programs to permit the orderly replacement of British officers by Malayans, but further discussion of this subject must be delayed until the following chapter.

III. The Role of the Colonial Bureaucracy in Malayan Development

(1) *Approach to Development*

In generalizing about the character of the involvement of the British in Malayan political and economic development, a distinction is customarily drawn between the Straits Settlements and the Native States. Rupert Emerson, in his brilliant study of Malaya and the East Indies that has yet to be superseded,[27] correctly draws a distinction between the "direct" rule of the Straits Settlements and the "indirect rule" of the Malay States. Yet in the economic development of the Peninsula, and to a lesser extent in its political development, the distinction is more apparent than real. Economic modernization was largely indirect (to retain the accepted terminology) in both areas, whereas the creation of alien political institutions primarily involved more direct intervention, though it must be admitted that the tactics varied somewhat, depending upon the political status of the area.

In a statement made only four years after the creation of the Federated Malay States, the Acting Resident-General, W. H. Treacher, outlined the indirect approach to economic advancement in Malaya that was to characterize British administration for the next half-century:

The general policy of the British advisers has been to interfere as little as possible with the manners, customs, methods and prejudices of the different nationalities composing the population of the States; to interfere not at all in matters touching the Mohammadan religion—the religion of the Malays; to attract capital—European, Chinese and other; to encourage the immigration of Chinese, Indian and other labourers; to assist the development of the mineral and agricultural resources of

27. *Malaysia: A Study in Direct and Indirect Rule* (New York: Macmillan and Company, 1937).

the States by making roads wherever the necessity for them was apparent, by constructing railways, by works of drainage and irrigation; by establishing security for life and property, by constructing Courts of Justice, by opening free hospitals and schools, by giving good titles to lands and by abolishing import duties (except opium and spirits) and all restraints on trade, commerce and industry.[28]

Beginning in Perak under the provisions of the Treaty of Pangkor of 1874, British colonial officers set about to introduce law and order into the potentially wealthy but strife-ridden western states of the Peninsula. Thereafter, and particularly after the Treaty of Federation, the present-day economic pattern was created. Hand-in-hand with this went the development of the still used communication and transportation networks, the creation of the lineal ancestors of today's medical and social services, the beginnings of the present educational system (together with the problems engendered by the system), and the establishment of the patterns that the contemporary judicial, financial, and administrative structures have followed.

(2) *Tin and Rubber*

British encouragement of private investment in Malaya had an almost immediate effect, and the extraction of natural resources was to combine with the development of a major cash crop to

28. Straits Settlements, *Report on the Federated Malay States, 1900* (London: HMSO, 1901), p. 7 (Cd. 815). A similarity may be noted here in the work of W. Arthur Lewis. Lewis lists nine categories of functions appropriate for government in the process of economic growth: maintaining public services, influencing attitudes, shaping economic institutions, influencing the use of resources, influencing the distribution of income, controlling the quantity of money, controlling fluctuations, ensuring full employment, and influencing the level of investment. Specifically, in the category of public services, Lewis argues that "the primary function of government is to maintain law and order. To this time has added other services—roads, schools, public health, surveys, research, and so on and on in a constantly growing list." See his *The Theory of Economic Growth* (London: Allen and Unwin, 1955). Joseph J. Spengler has suggested that "the contributions that the bureaucracy can make to economic development are of three fairly distinct sorts. First, it can help to establish and strengthen what we have called . . . the minimum legal and public-service pre-conditions to economic development, namely, law and order and security in general, infra-structural elements, money and banking institutions, and a legal and administrative structure favorable to the conduct of economic activities by both domestic and foreign enterprise." See "Bureaucracy and Economic Development," in Joseph LaPalombara, ed., *Bureaucracy and Political Development* (Princeton: Princeton University Press, 1963), pp. 199–232, at 225.

Although a few short latitudinal lines were also built, the second period of railway construction (1896–1909) was marked chiefly by the opening of longer north-south lines that one by one connected the interior terminal points of the railways in the various mining districts. In 1909 the Federated Malay States Railways completed the construction of a line for the Johore State Railway linking the FMSR with Johore Bahru, and thence by ferry with Singapore.[34] Thus, by the close of this second period of railway construction there were more than 500 miles of open line, and it was possible to travel and ship goods by train from Johore Bahru, opposite Singapore, to Prai, opposite Penang, a distance of some 465 miles.

The final stage in the development of the Malayan railway system began with the construction of the Kedah railway in 1912 (completed in 1918) and ended with the completion of the East Coast Railway in 1931. It was during this period that the FMSR reached its maximum stage of development and the whole rail complex was tied together into an integrated system. The greatest achievement of the period was the opening of the East Coast to rail travel by the construction of a single track cutting off from the trunk route at Gemas on the Johore-Negri Sembilan border, proceeding roughly northward for some 475 miles through the states of Pahang and Kelantan, and terminating at Tumpat, north of Kota Bharu. The Singapore Government Railway, which began operating on the island in 1903, was purchased by the FMSR in 1913, and a decade later the island's railways were organically connected with the trunk route of the FMSR by the construction of the causeway across the Johore Straits. In the north, the extension of the Kedah railway through Perlis to Padang Besar and the construction of the Pasir Mas-Rantau Panjang branch in Kelantan tied the FMSR in with the Siamese railways on both the East and West Coasts of the Peninsula.

---

heart of the Valley by the completion of the north-south Tapah Road–Bata Gajah–Ipoh line. The first railway in Malaya was actually built by Ceylon government engineers and handed over upon completion to the Perak government. The Port Dickson–Seramban line was the only railroad in Malaya built and operated by a private company.

34. The FMSR was created through the amalgamation of the Perak State Railway and the Selangor State Railway. The FMSR also leased and operated the Johore State Railway.

As the following table demonstrates, in the three decades between the turn of the century and the completion of the East Coast railway in 1931, the length of open track in the Peninsula multiplied almost four-fold. While the first and second stages in the development of these railways were associated primarily with the growth of the tin mining industry, during the final period it was the rubber industry that benefited most from the availability of rail service. Railways may have been built originally to serve the tin-mining areas, but, as even a cursory study of a land utilization map will prove, rubber estates tended to follow the north-south trunk routes of the FMSR.[35]

Table 11. *Railway Mileage, Pan-Malayan, 1902–39* *

Year	Mileage	Year	Mileage
1902	274	1914	822
1904	339	1916	876
1906	428	1918	949
1908	468	1920	1014
1910	538	1930	1074
1912	734	1939	1068

* This table has been compiled chiefly from the *Annual Reports* of the Straits Settlements and the Federated Malay States for the period.

During the period of prewar British colonialism it was the intent of the administration to disrupt the traditional institutions of government as little as possible, and thus considerable emphasis was placed upon the fiction of indirect rule, a doctrine that was

35. In the southern half of the Peninsula rubber lands lie generally between the trunk line and the West Coast, a distance inland that seldom exceeds fifty miles. In the northwest the trunk line, somewhat nearer to the coast than in the south, almost bisects the rubber areas in northwest Perak, Kedah, and Province Wellesley. The few rubber holdings of central Malaya generally parallel the Gemas-Kelantan railway from the Pahang-Negri Sembilan border of the vicinity of Kuala Lipis. North of Kuala Krai the railway bisects the rubber estates of Kelantan, where the Duff Development Company pioneered the planting of rubber beginning in 1900. An excellent land utilization map, on which the preceding analysis is based, was prepared by the Survey Department of the Federation of Malaya in 1954 and is appended as a fold-out section in Federation of Malaya, *The Land Administration Commission, Report* (Kuala Lumpur: Government Press, 1958). The *Report* itself is extremely valuable, and the presence of the map considerably enhances its usefulness.

elevated to dogma by Lugard in Nigeria.[36] There is no doubt that the existing hierarchy was preserved, and indeed strengthened, by British colonial policies; yet it would be a most serious error to equate these facts to the supposition that indirect rule preserved the traditional society.[37] As the Peninsula was opened up to access by the railways, economic penetration followed (or in some cases preceded it and provided the stimulation for the ensuing railway development), and as the Peninsula was developed economically the demand for expanded governmental services grew. Mosquito control, surveying, land codes, education—all of these may have been built around the existing social hierarchy, but at the same time each contributed in part to the destruction of the traditional ordering of values and to their partial replacement by an alien standard. The Oxford or Cambridge educated District Officer serving in the *ulu* far from Kuala Lumpur might have been instructed to respect local customs and practices, and he may even have tried scrupulously to obey these instructions; yet, in the end he, and the hundreds of other government servants like him, were the agents by which momentous changes were introduced into the country. That the number of colonial officers in Malaya grew rapidly as railways opened the country cannot be doubted. Consider, for example, the increase among selected services during the two decades between 1913 and 1932, as illustrated in Table 12 below.

Table 12. *FMS: Growth of Selected Services, 1913–32* *

Year	MCS	Education	Legal	Medical	Police	Public works
1913	129	14	6	68	33	64
1932	256	147	11	174	124	126 †

* This table was compiled from the *Civil Lists* of the FMS for the years indicated.
† This figure is based on the 1934 total.

During the period of rapid change in the first three decades of the twentieth century cause and effect became almost indis-

36. See Lord Lugard, *The Dual Mandate in Tropical Africa* (London: William Blackwood and Sons Ltd., 1926).
37. On traditional Malayan society, see chap. i, above.

tinguishable one from the other. The economic demand for increased services produced deeper social changes and these social changes in turn brought about a demand for more services. As urbanization gained momentum, communications became more intense and penetrated to a lower level of the society. The first telephone exchanges were installed in Kuala Lumpur in 1897 and in Ipoh and Taiping in 1902. In 1906 posts and telegraph functions in each of the states were combined into a Federal Department, and in 1909 an overland telegraph wire from Penang to Singapore completed the rudimentary integration of communications within the Straits Settlements and the FMS. In the three decades of rapid development, as the following table shows, telephone and telegraph lines in the Federated Malay States alone multiplied almost twenty-fold.

Table 13. *FMS: Telephone and Telegraph Service, 1903–35* *

Year	Total wire mileage (1000 miles)	Year	Total wire mileage (1000 miles)
1903	1.8	1923	16.4
1907	3.1	1927	21.7
1911	6.2	1931	24.3
1915	9.8	1935	31.2
1919	11.8		

* This table has been compiled from the *Annual Reports* of the Federated Malay States for the period.

(4) *Education*

British educational policies in Malaya were as liberal as those of other Southeast Asian colonial powers,[38] though the communal imbalance permitted by the colonial administration was to be the eventual source of considerable difficulty for dependent as well as independent Malaya. The first Inspector of Schools was appointed in Perak in 1890 and in the FMS in 1897. Malay College opened in January, 1905, a subject which will be treated in more

38. For a convenient summary of educational policies and practices, see Brian Harrison, *South-East Asia* (London: Macmillan and Co., 1955), pp. 227–31.

detail in a later chapter, and a Director of Education for the Straits Settlements and the FMS was created the following year.[39] As Table 14 demonstrates, the number of schools in colonial Malaya grew rapidly between the time of Federation and the coming of World War II.

Table 14. *FMS: Government and Government-Aided Schools, 1891–1936* *

Year	Number of schools	Average enrollment (1000)
1891	91	4.0
1896	150	6.6
1900	195	8.1
1906	285	16.9
1910	356	22.0
1916	480	28.1
1921	583	39.7
1924	683	47.2
1936	1452	95.2

* This table has been compiled from statistics presented in the *Annual Reports* of the Straits Settlements and the Federated Malay States for the period covered.

The impact of education affected the course of Malayan development both positively and negatively. On the one hand, British-sponsored education, particularly the English-language education, provided the means for achieving vertical social mobility and thus in a very direct manner was responsible for the creation of a Westernized elite that today permeates both the bureaucratic and political fields. On the other hand, the corresponding neglect of Chinese education by the British contributed to the separateness of the immigrant community and in no small measure prevented free communication among the several groups. The fol-

39. See Straits Settlements, *Report on the Federated Malay States, 1901* (London: HMSO, 1902), p. 20 (Cd. 1297); *ibid.*, *1905* (London: HMSO, 1905), p. 16 (Cd. 3186); Ho Seng Ong, *Education for Unity in Malaya* (Penang: Malayan Teachers' Union, 1952), pp. 43–46; and Hubert S. Banner, "The Growth of Education in Malaya," *The Asiatic Review*, XXVIII (Jan., 1932), 103–7.

lowing table is revealing and goes far toward explaining many of the communal problems that Malaya still faces today.

Table 15. *FMS: Distribution of Schools, 1921, According to Language of Instruction* *

English		
Government	Government-aided, boys	Government-aided, girls
11	19	11
(1,869 students)	(5,991 students)	(2,122 students)

Malay (All government schools)	
boys	girls
346	56
(19,954 students)	(1,911 students)

Tamil		Chinese †	
Government	Government-aided	Government	Government-aided
10	99	1	0

* This table has been derived from statistics contained in Federated Malay States, *Report for 1921 on the Federated Malay States* (London: HMSO, 1922), p. 17.
† In addition to the single government school, there were approximately 90 fully private Chinese schools in 1921.

IV. Conclusion

The British colonial bureaucracy was the agency by which political and economic modernization were introduced into the Peninsula, and the details of these contacts are history.[40] What is important for our purposes here is the manner in which the Malayan society and economy were reshaped and the role of the bureaucracy in this process. Before the intervention of Europeans, Malaya was made up of tradition-directed monarchies

40. For an uncritical summary of the British contribution to the development of Malaya by a former colonial servant, see S. W. Jones, *Public Administration in Malaya* (London: Royal Institute of International Affairs, 1952).

ruling with varying degrees of absolutism over kingdoms often beset by internal turmoil, subject to the hygienic hazards of tropical life, and subsisting on a primitive agricultural economy. On the eve of World War II Malaya was producing a major portion of the world's tin and rubber; it could boast of a superior transportation and communications network; it possessed a sophisticated administrative system of seldom questioned integrity and efficiency; and the country already contained in embryo the major institutions of government found in present-day Malaya.

Yet all coins have two sides, and it would be unrealistic to conclude this chapter without pointing out some of the problems engendered by colonial policies and the colonial bureaucratic structure. British educational policies have already been mentioned, but should perhaps be pursued a bit further. There can be little doubt that the absence of government-supervised education might have been at least one of the major factors contributing to the separateness of the Chinese community, but it would probably be an error to look for a colonial plot behind this. There is no evidence in official records that this was a part of any preconceived policy of "divide and rule," a cliché that has already been rejected in the preceding chapter. Primarily, educational policies seemed to be creatures of economic forces: the Chinese were adequately self-sufficient to provide for their own education, and the British were content to let them do it in the interests of holding down governmental expenditures, which were always threatening to get out of hand. Whether education alone could better have integrated the Chinese into a colonial society that was intentionally Malay in outlook is now an academic question, but there seems little doubt that more far-sighted educational policies would at least have made the communications process less cumbersome. Better communications between the British and the Chinese in turn might have reduced the areas of misunderstanding that arose after World War II.[41]

The transportation and communications network that emerged under colonial rule was inferior to few, and perhaps none, in

41. See chap. i, n. 55 for an example of the reluctance to face the communications problem.

Southeast Asia.[42] Yet, while its economic basis may have been sound, it contributed little to the political integration of pre-1946 Malaya. The network did not provide a centripetal force for integrating the inherently unnatural Federated Malay States; it left the East Coast politically isolated until late in the period of colonial rule; and the network focused not on the Federal Capital of Kuala Lumpur, but on the colonial capital of Singapore. The influence of these factors is still apparent today. The politics of the East Coast, the only area where the political strength of the traditionalist Pan-Malayan Islamic Party is a serious threat to the Alliance Government, reflect the relative superficiality of Western contacts; and the attempted separation of Singapore from the Peninsula after World War II threatened an economic and political disruption that was serious enough to cause the leaders of both areas to have second thoughts.

On the eve of World War II the British colonial bureaucracy was staffed in the senior posts almost exclusively by expatriates. It was no doubt providing "good government" for Malaya, but it was "good" as defined by the colonial power. Most important, from the postwar Malay point of view, however, was the fact that it was expatriate and not indigenous in composition. It was realized by both the rulers and the ruled that this was a feature of Malayan bureaucracy that soon must change and that the change must be dramatic.

42. Fisher, *op. cit.*, p. 134, provides the following comparative statistics for the year 1939:

Country	Mileage	Area per railway mile (square miles)	Population per railway mile (1000)
British Malaya	1,068	49	5.2
Netherlands Indies	4,589	160	15.3
French Indo-China	1,817	152	13.0

3

The Transitional Phase

When Malaya gained its independence in 1957 the country enjoyed the services of a highly sophisticated and unquestionably efficient bureaucratic apparatus. Yet in most respects it was still a "colonial bureaucracy," for it was largely staffed by expatriate officers. To be sure, from the time of the introduction of the member system of government in 1955 the bureaucracy had come increasingly under the direction of the Legislative and Executive Councils and less subject to the guidance of the Colonial Office, but so long as British officials remained prominent in the hierarchy the administrative structure bore an uneasy resemblance to the old colonial service. British and Malayan leaders were in agreement that the expatriate officers should be replaced through indigenous recruitment, and the resulting process of "Malayanization" will be the central focus of the present chapter.

I. The Malayanization Scheme

Of course "Malayanization" in the broadest sense did not suddenly emerge as an immediate pre-independence phenomenon. The Malay Administrative Service, a subject discussed in a later chapter, was itself a product of an attempt to economize in the administration of the country by recruiting local officers to staff the subordinate administrative posts.[1] Even the creation of the MAS in 1910 might be antedated, however, for it was in 1896, at the time of the creation of the Federated Malay States, that the first suggestion was put forward that local officers might well take

1. On the MAS, see chap. v, below.

over the minor administrative posts then held by expatriates.[2] Yet these early attempts to recruit local officers were sporadic and the goal in each case was to supplement the expatriate civil servants, not to supplant them. In these respects the Malayanization program enunciated shortly before independence differed greatly from earlier moves to recruit Malayan officers.

Although the Malayanization scheme was first considered specifically in the London Constitutional Conference of 1956, the guidelines had been laid down by Colonial No. 306 of 1954. The Colonial Office in 1954 had proposed that any government gaining political independence from Great Britain should undertake to guarantee the following:

1. Terms and conditions of service of expatriate officers should not be less favorable than those enjoyed prior to independence;

2. Pensions should be safeguarded;

3. H. M. Government should continue to regard the expatriate officers as H. M. servants even after they had passed into the employ of the new state;

4. Any reasonable request for transfer should be accepted and should not disturb the officer's pension rights;

5. Expatriates should be considered on equal terms with local officers in matters of promotion;

6. Expatriates should be given adequate notice of the termination of employment, and H.M. Government should then strive to find the officers alternative employment; and

7. In the event of premature retirement at the hands of the new government, expatriate officers should receive adequate compensation for the interruption of their careers.[3]

The first question facing the London Conference in matters of Malayanization was the rate at which the scheme should proceed. The first Malayanization Committee, established in 1954 in Kuala Lumpur, had argued that the replacement of expatriates by lo-

2. See Federated Malay States, *Correspondence Respecting the Federation of the Protected Malay States* (Taiping, Perak: Government Printing Office, 1896), p. 9.
3. Great Britain, Colonial Office, *Reorganization of the Colonial Service* (London: HMSO, 1954), p. 4 (Col. No. 306). These provisions have been paraphrased and summarized in the above statements.

cally recruited officers should take place only as normal attrition occurred. Any accelerated recruitment, the Committee reasoned, would endanger the promotion prospects of Division II officers, produce periods of stagnation in later years, and saturate the bureaucracy with servants probably less competent than later applicants.[4] By 1956, however, it was apparent that any scheme based on retirement by normal attrition would be unpopular, and the London Conference therefore agreed that a principle of premature retirement might be instituted provided the guidelines of Colonial No. 306 were observed.

The second Malayanization Committee, appointed following the London Conference, adhered to the recommendations of the Conference. Arguing that a public service "is more than a rapidly assembled aggregate of competent individuals," the Committee recommended that the principle of premature retirement of expatriates should be observed, but that it should be tempered by the practice of retaining expatriates until fully qualified Malayans were in fact available to fill the posts.[5]

Within this broad policy of accelerated but controlled Malayanization certain time periods were imposed, for total Malayanization was to take place in three phases. Part I included twenty-three departmental services, or cadres within particular departments, which were scheduled for Malayanization no later than July 1, 1960. Part II (seventeen services) was projected for complete Malayanization by January 1, 1962. Part III was made up chiefly of technical and professional personnel for whom replacements were not available in sufficient numbers and whose target date was therefore delayed until 1965.[6]

The details of the Malayanization scheme were spelled out in

4. Federation of Malaya, *Report of the Committee on the Malayanization of the Government Service* (Kuala Lumpur: Government Press, 1954), p. 6.
5. Two major documents were produced by the second Malayanization Committee: Federation of Malaya, *Malayanization of the Public Service: A Statement of Policy* (Kuala Lumpur: Government Press, 1956); and Federation of Malaya, *Report of the Committee on the Malayanization of the Public Service* (Kuala Lumpur: Government Press, 1956). The former document is a summary statement of the policy provisions detailed in the final *Report*.
6. For a small additional group of expatriates replacements were immediately available and Malayanization was therefore to take place as soon as convenient. A number of these were actually Malayanized prior to independence.

the Tenth Schedule of the *Federation of Malaya Agreement,* appended by law in 1956 to the Federation Agreement of 1948.[7] Each "entitled officer"[8] was required to state in writing prior to July 1, 1957, his desire to remain in the service of the independent Federation or to retire under the financial provisions of the scheme immediately. Within two months thereafter the Federation Government replied in writing to those indicating a desire to stay, either inviting them to remain or pointing out that their services were not needed.[9] Those invited to continue in service were at the same time informed of the approximate period of time that their services would be desired, and on the basis of this information each officer decided on remaining or leaving. Any officer who accepted the period proposed by the Government continued to serve in the independent Federation on the same terms and conditions of service under which he was recruited to the Colonial Service. An expatriate could retire at any time after giving six months' notice to the Government, but the Government, for its part, was obligated to retain the officer for the entire period of guaranteed service. By law, expatriate officers enjoyed the same promotion opportunities after independence as did their Asian colleagues, though in fact it was the common practice of the Public Services Commission to permit indigenous officers to jump their expatriate superiors.[10] However, in the light of the

7. See Federation of Malaya, *The Federation of Malaya Agreement (Amendment No. 4) Ordinance, 1956* (Kuala Lumpur: Government Press, 1958), No. 9 of 1956. Similar and complementary statutes were passed by the Second Legislative Council several months prior to the enactment of the Tenth Schedule. See Federation of Malaya, *Federal Ordinances and State and Settlement Enactments, 1956* (Kuala Lumpur: Government Press, 1958), No. 17 of 1956, "Pensions (Entitled Officers) Ordinance, 1956"; and *ibid.,* No. 21 of 1956, "Entitled Officers (Gratuities) Ordinance, 1956." These ordinances preceded the Tenth Schedule and were repealed when the more comprehensive Schedule came into effect. See Federation of Malaya, *Federal Ordinances and State and Settlement Enactments, 1957* (Kuala Lumpur: Government Press, 1959), No. 28 of 1957, "Pensions (Entitled Officers) and Entitled Officers (Gratuities) (Repeal) Ordinance, 1957."

8. An "entitled officer" (a shorthand form of "officer entitled to Malayanization compensation") is one who was on the pensionable establishment, or on probation for the pensionable establishment, on or after the "operative date" (July 1, 1957). The term "entitled officer" is in common usage in Malaya and will be retained here for convenience.

9. To the author's knowledge, most officers indicating a desire to serve after independence were invited to remain at their posts.

10. This guarantee of equal treatment for expatriate officers was agreed informally at first and later incorporated formally into Federation of Malaya, *The*

requirements of Malayanization this practice permitted a smoother transition than would have been possible had the final period of the expatriates' service resembled a great game of musical chairs with each officer moving up one step as the more senior officers disappeared from the top. Moreover, the inevitability of such discrimination seemed to be accepted philosophically and with good humor by most expatriates.

The provisions of Malayanization are skewed in such a manner as to make it attractive for expatriates to spend the maximum time possible in Malaya. Loss-of-career compensation is paid to all entitled officers. The sum paid is based on the officer's annual pensionable emolument multiplied by a factor derived from tables based on the officer's age and length of service, with the limitation that no sum can exceed £11,000.[11] To prevent the expected exodus of experienced officers, the financial provisions of Malayanization stipulated that compensation for each officer in service should be calculated from the date after July 1, 1957, most advantageous in each case. Thus, expatriates need not leave at the point that the factor reaches its maximum in order to enjoy the most liberal Malayanization benefits.[12]

The cost of the Malayanization program to the Federation Government, which has borne the total expense, has been great. The last figures available indicate that with about 80 per cent of the expatriate officers retired as of January 1, 1962, the cost

---

Federation of Malaya and United Kingdom Public Officers Agreement, 1959 (Kuala Lumpur: Government Press, 1959) (Cmd. 14 of 1959).

11. The Table of Factors for computing loss of career compensation was appended to the Tenth Schedule of the *Federation of Malaya Agreement, 1948.* The maximum factor (4.96) occurred in the case of an entitled officer thirty-nine years of age with eight or more years service.

12. Malayanized officers also retain pension benefits identical to those enjoyed by pre-Merdeka civil servants, the only difference being that all Malayanized officers are entitled to such benefits regardless of the length of time they have served in Malaya. (Officers retiring before independence were required to have completed at least ten years of pensionable service before becoming eligible for these benefits.) Mention might also be made of officers who leave Malaya through transfers after the beginning of Malayanization. In such cases the Federation does not pay loss of career compensation, but it does pay a lump-sum payment to each officer if the post to which he is transferred pays a salary inferior to that of his Malayan assignment. The amount paid is equal to five times the difference of the two salaries for officers up to a maximum of fifty years of age. For officers between fifty-one and fifty-five the multiplier is the difference between the officer's age and the retirement age of fifty-five.

to the government in the payment of loss of career compensation alone had been more than $15 million,[13] and it has been suggested informally that this total might eventually reach or exceed $23 million. Moreover, this represents only direct expenses and does not take into consideration the financial outlay necessary to train Malayans to fill the posts vacated by Europeans.[14]

II. The Statistical Results of Malayanization

The following summary illustrates well the departure of expatriates from Malaya and the numerical transition from a colonial to an independent bureaucracy.[15]

Table 16. *The Malayanization of the Senior Bureaucracy, 1956–62*

	Entitled officers remaining
May, 1956	2,060
July, 1957	1,564
January, 1958	936
January, 1959	736
January, 1960	555
January, 1962	382
July, 1962	200 (estimated)

The change in the composition of the Malayan Civil Service has provided one of the most dramatic evidences of the results of the Malayanization program. At the beginning of the operative period (July 1, 1957) expatriate officers staffed 67 per cent of all MCS posts. As of January 1, 1962, only twenty-six European officers appeared in the MCS *Staff List* (9.2 per cent), and it is reported that as of January 1, 1963, this figure has been reduced

13. This figure has been derived by tabulating the *Federal Estimates* for the period.

14. The figures have now begun to diminish, but in previous years the Federation Government has expended approximately one million dollars annually on training related to the Malayanization program. In 1961 the expenditure dropped to about $650,000.

15. These figures are based on unpublished statistics provided the author by the Federation Establishment Office, Kuala Lumpur.

to less than ten. In the bureaucracy as a whole the change is not so dramatic, but it is certainly significant. In May, 1956, Europeans held 71.2 per cent of all Division I posts; about a half-decade later (January 1, 1962) the European segment of the bureaucracy had been reduced to 14.1 per cent.[16]

It is apparent that significant changes have been taking place in the composition of the Malayan bureaucracy, if only by the evidence of the disappearance of Europeans, but a more significant fact is revealed by a closer examination of indigenous recruitment to replace the departing expatriates. It is a frequent assertion, both in Malaya and abroad, that the senior bureaucracy of the Federation is almost the preserved domain of the Malays. If one considers the senior bureaucracy to be Division I as a whole—the approach that is generally accepted—then the assertion cannot be supported by statistical research. Table 17, which is illustrated graphically on page 70, summarizes the growth of the various communal groups in the senior bureaucracy.[17]

16. It should also be pointed out this is a true reflection of the actual size of the European official community in Malaya since the number of officers serving on contract is negligible. Unlike Nigeria, for example, Malayanized officers are barred by law from returning to government service on contract. In fact, it has become increasingly difficult for Malayanized officers to return to Malaya even to accept commercial employment.

17. The tables employed throughout this chapter reflect many of the problems connected with the gathering of statistical data in Malaya. Statistics are seldom available for the researcher simply to record, and it is therefore usually left to his ingenuity to compile them from whatever sources might be available. The single exception occurs in the case of the quarterly Malayanization statistics, which have been carefully recorded until recently by the Pensions Division of the FEO. In tabulating the annual *Staff Lists*, which are the only sources of information available on the communal composition of the senior bureaucracy, the statistical hazards of Malayan research become apparent. However carefully the necessary tabulations are done, and regardless of the number of rechecks, the results are sometimes less than satisfactory. Note the following discrepancies between the official Malayanization statistics and the tally of expatriate officers derived from the official *Staff Lists* for the same dates:

	Malayanization statistics	Staff List *Tally*
January 1, 1958	936	1,200
January 1, 1959	736	1,004
January 1, 1960	555	657
January 1, 1962	382	409

This apparently large discrepancy can be explained in part by the time lag between the two sets of figures. So far as the Service Division of the FEO (where the *Staff Lists* are compiled) is concerned, an expatriate is on the establishment until he has used all leave time accrued and is actually off the regular payroll of the Federation Government. On the other hand, the Pensions Division of the FEO drops all expatriate officers from its list as soon as they have physically de-

Table 17. *Communal Representation in the Senior Bureaucracy, 1957–62* *

	1957		1958		1959		1960		1962	
	No.	*%*	*No.*	*%*	*No.*	*%*	*No.*	*%*	*No.*	*%*
Expatriate	1,687	61.0	1,200	45.0	1,004	36.4	657	24.6	409	14.1
Malay	390	14.1	513	19.4	653	23.6	737	27.6	850	29.3
Chinese	366	13.2	520	19.5	660	23.8	750	28.1	987	34.0
Indian	191	7.0	266	10.0	326	11.8	384	14.4	462	15.9
Other	127	4.6	166	6.2	120	4.3	143	5.4	194	6.7
Total	2,761		2,665		2,763		2,671		2,902	

* This table has been derived by the author by tabulating the annual *Staff Lists* prepared by the Service Division of the Federation Establishment Office for the years indicated. The date is January 1 for each of the years.

Graph 1. *The Malayanization of the Senior Bureaucracy*

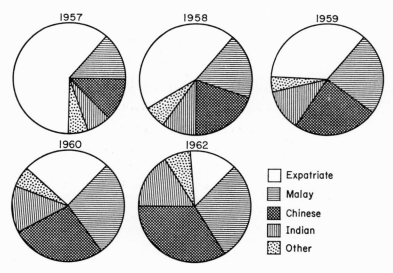

It seems that Chinese were well represented in the senior bureaucracy even at the time of independence, and since then they have been recruited into the senior services at a considerably

parted from Malaya. The difference between these might vary in individual cases by several months, but this does not seem adequate to explain all discrepancies.

greater rate than have either of the other two indigenous communities. Table 18 shows that the Malay segment of the non-European senior bureaucracy has actually declined 2.1 per cent during the five-year period 1957–62, at the same time that the Chinese and Indian segments have increased 5.6 and 0.8 per cent respectively.

Table 18. *Total Non-European Senior Bureaucracy: Comparative Recruitment by Communities, 1957 and 1962* *

	Malay		Chinese		Indian	
	No.	%	No.	%	No.	%
1957	390	36.2	366	34.0	191	17.8
1962	850	34.1	987	39.6	462	18.6

* The category "other" has been omitted here.

While the Indian community may appear to be just holding its own in the bureaucracy, in fact the relative increase has been considerably greater than these absolute figures suggest. During the five year period 1957–62 the Indian community of an age to be employed in the senior bureaucracy (25–55) declined from 12.7 per cent to 10.2 per cent of the total Malayan population of this age group.[18] Viewed in these relative terms—that is, based on the numbers of the major communities falling within the age span of the senior bureaucracy—the Malays in 1957 held bureaucratic posts equaling 71 per cent of their community's proportion of the population, and in 1962 this figure had fallen to 67 per cent. Comparable figures for the Chinese, on the other hand, were

18. The Malay and Chinese communities of the age span 25–55 have also declined, but by almost identical percentages. The Malays of this group constituted 51.3 per cent in 1957 and 51.0 per cent in 1962. For the Chinese, these figures are 34.4 and 34.1. These figures have been derived by tabulating the age group 25–55 on the basis of the 1957 *Census Report* and the projections provided based on medium fertility. See Federation of Malaya, *1957 Population Census, Report No. 14* (Kuala Lumpur: Department of Statistics, 1962), Tables 7.14A and 7.14B. Under normal conditions it would have been more accurate to reduce the upper age limits considerably since officers would seldom have been recruited into the senior bureaucracy late in their careers; however, the demands of the Malayanization program have occasioned a large number of promotions of older civil servants from the subordinate services, and these are often men nearing the retirement age.

99 per cent and 117 per cent.[19] Even excluding the predominantly Chinese medical services,[20] which it might be argued are only accidentally a part of the bureaucracy, the Chinese today hold slightly more posts than their comparable percentage of the total age group, while the Malays fall about one-fifth below this level. Similarly, viewing recruitment during the five-year period, the Chinese and Indians have both gained considerably larger portions of the senior bureaucracy while the Malays have relatively lost ground.

Table 19. *Total Non-European Senior Bureaucracy, Less Medical Services, 1957 and 1962*

	1957		1962			
	Number of posts held	*Percentage of total posts*	*Number of posts held*	*Percentage of total posts*	*Absolute loss/gain*	*Relative* * *loss/gain*
Malay	352	46.5	772	41.5	−5.0	−4.7
Chinese	215	28.6	640	34.4	+5.8	+6.1
Indian	119	15.8	318	17.1	+1.3	+3.8

* Adjusted to reflect relative changes in the sizes of the age span 25–55. See note 18, above. Loss/gain figures are given in percentages. The small category "other" has been omitted here.

While statistics might prove that the non-Malay communities are far better represented in the senior bureaucracy than has been recognized, it is equally apparent that the distribution of the communities throughout the services is uneven and that in terms of prestige, recognition, and sometimes actual power, the services are not all equal regardless of the general equality of present-day salary scales. On the whole, the Chinese and Indians have tended to gravitate toward the technical and professional services, while the Malays are centered largely in the administrative and police services. The following five tables illustrate well the uneven dis-

19. That is to say, $X = \dfrac{N}{PN_t}$, where X = the percentage of the expected share of posts actually held, N = the actual number of posts held, P = the community's percentage of the total age span 25–55, and N_t = the total number of non-expatriate posts.

20. On the communal composition of the medical services, see Table 21 below.

tribution of the communal groups in several of the major services of the senior bureaucracy.

Table 20. *Malayan Civil Service, by Community, 1957–62*

	1957	1958	1959	1960	1962
Expatriate	220	154	104	55	26
Malay	128	123	166	195	219
Chinese	9	11	13	16	17
Indian	3	4	9	12	15

Table 21. *Medical Services, by Community, 1957–62*

	1957	1958	1959	1960	1962
Expatriate	130	90	86	69	31
Malay	38	42	52	53	78
Chinese	151	196	224	268	347
Indian	72	80	93	113	144

Table 22. *Police Services, by Community, 1957–62*

	1957	1958	1959	1960	1962
Expatriate	374	231	161	108	52
Malay	92	142	150	146	171
Chinese	50	87	96	96	124
Indian	37	67	68	78	80

Table 23. *Education Services, by Community, 1957–62*

	1957	1958	1959	1960	1962
Expatriate	133	111	105	66	54
Malay	9	30	67	71	74
Chinese	47	62	105	108	131
Indian	22	35	59	54	64

Table 24. *Public Works Department Services, by Community,* *1957–62*

	1957	1958	1959	1960	1962
Expatriate	207	157	155	84	71
Malay	11	21	25	32	35
Chinese	11	25	44	49	75
Indian	6	12	17	21	27

The above tables demonstrate the strongholds of the various communities in individual services, but it is also revealing to classify the bureaucracy according to the type of educational experience necessary to satisfy recruitment qualifications.[21] Though such a breakdown must be arbitrary in some of the relatively minor services, it seems possible to divide the bureaucracy on this basis into four components: 1. Services requiring a general educational background (often, but certainly not invariably, implying the attainment of a university degree in the liberal arts). 2. Technical and professional services requiring a background in the natural, physical, engineering, medical, or mathematical sciences. 3. Technical and professional services requiring a background in subjects such as law, architecture, education, etc. 4. Non-professional services, such as police, customs, immigration, postal, etc., drawing usually but not invariably from the educational streams of components 1 and 3, and occasionally requiring somewhat lower educational qualifications. The following four tables demonstrate the Malayanization of the total bureaucracy on the basis of these categories.[22]

21. It would be tempting to employ the categories generally found in official reports—"administrative; professional and technical; and non-professional." However, such a system of classification is not entirely satisfactory since it fails to distinguish between, for example, judges and nurses—two posts that may both be "professional" but that draw from different educational streams. Similarly, the only senior "administrative" service is the Malayan Civil Service, but there are many minor senior services that draw from Malayans with educational backgrounds similar to those of MCS recruits. For this reason the official categories have not been adopted in Tables 25 and 26.

22. It has been necessary to omit several very minor services, totaling less than twenty persons per year, when it proved impossible to determine the precise nature of the requisite qualifications. The small category "other" has also been omitted.

Table 25. *Bureaucracy Requiring General Educational Background (Category One), by Community, 1957-62*

	1957	1958	1959	1960	1962
Expatriate	296	210	152	91	44
Malay	154	160	209	252	286
Chinese	47	64	70	81	98
Indian	23	27	36	41	52

Table 26. *Technical and Professional Bureaucracy: Scientific Background (Category Two), by Community, 1957-62*

	1957	1958	1959	1960	1962
Expatriate	653	482	453	303	200
Malay	78	102	130	145	183
Chinese	195	259	331	391	539
Indian	90	108	135	168	215

Table 27. *Technical and Professional Bureaucracy: Non-Scientific Background (Category Three), by Community, 1957-62*

	1957	1958	1959	1960	1962
Expatriate	215	168	165	106	88
Malay	18	45	93	104	115
Chinese	62	82	132	141	176
Indian	32	48	70	69	89

Table 28. *Non-Professional Bureaucracy (Category Four), by Community, 1957-62*

	1957	1958	1959	1960	1962
Expatriate	513	333	224	152	73
Malay	138	201	209	229	260
Chinese	60	113	123	128	164
Indian	45	82	83	99	102

As the tables above show, the Malays have vastly disproportionate representation in category one, and the Chinese, in
category two, which suggests certain trends in higher education
in Malaya.[23] There are of course legal bars blocking the entry of
Chinese and Indians into the MCS, the major service in category
one; therefore some potential non-Malay members of this category are channeled into other services. At the same time, it is
probable that the Malays, influenced by Malay College [24] (and
similar institutions) and following the British tradition of a liberal
general education, have been less inclined to pursue a technical
or professional education than have the Chinese and Indians.
Whatever the causes, the result seems to have been that the
Chinese have flocked to the services requiring a scientific background in great numbers, and the Malays have confined themselves chiefly to posts of a non-technical nature.

As of January 1, 1961, the most recent date for which statistics
of this nature are available, six of the eleven total services
scheduled for complete Malayanization had met the target
date; [25] three services had but a single expatriate officer each remaining; and two services had delayed the Malayanization of a
small group of officers when it became apparent that fully qualified local recruits were not available. Thus, of 416 officers
scheduled for Malayanization by mid-1960, only 61 remained in
the bureaucracy at the beginning of 1961. Although each
projected deadline may necessarily be approached with some
flexibility, the course of the Malayanization program to date suggests that the bureaucracy will virtually be an indigenous one as
the final phase comes to a close at the end of 1965. With only
about 200 expatriates remaining as of mid-1962 it is possible to
discern certain trends and problems inherent in the successful
Malayanization scheme.

23. Unfortunately, reliable educational statistics are not available to refute or
support these suggested correlations, but educational leaders in Malaya and Singapore in informal conversations have recognized the unbalanced distribution of
communities among fields within the sciences and those of the humanities.
24. On Malay College, see chap. v, below.
25. Twenty-three services were included under Part I of the Malayanization
schedule, but, of these, twelve represented particular groups within total services
and were not tallied separately on the Malayanization statistics.

III. The Complications of Malayanization

The Malayanization scheme has been expensive, but it probably represents a long-range bargain. By preventing a mass exodus of experienced personnel, it dulled the birth pains of the newly independent state and at the same time removed from the arena of possible controversy many potential sources of tension between the colonial power and the former colony. The program represents a compromise between two illogical extremes and was probably the most rational alternative available. Yet the Malayanization of the senior services has brought about new problems, some clearly foreseen, others largely unforeseen, and any appraisal that does not also include these complications would be unrealistic. The problems occasioned by Malayanization have been threefold: first, despite the criterion that Malayanization should take place only as qualified Malayans became available, there has probably been a general lowering of professional standards; second, unbalanced recruitment has produced problems for the future; and last, the nature of Malay society has produced some unexpected influences on the decision-making process.

To suggest that there has probably been a general lowering of professional standards is not to question the inherent ability of Malayans to staff posts formerly held by Europeans; it is only meant to point out that Malayan bureaucracy has been in a state of flux, and it is probably inevitable that standards should decline under such conditions. Officers have scarcely had an opportunity to become familiar with one job when the demands of Malayanization have pressed them into a new post with even more responsibility. Moreover, it is evident that technical posts in the senior bureaucracy are destined to be filled for many years by indigenous officers on the whole less qualified than their expatriate predecessors. Such competency is based on long periods of advanced specialized training, supplemented by practical experience, and this must be built upon a background of basic education that has prepared the student to undertake the necessary advanced study. Thus, to train personnel to fill such posts is a long-range undertaking that really begins at the primary-school level, and it therefore seems that for many years to come locally recruited officers will not have enjoyed the same educational and occupational advantages as those of their expatriate predecessors. At the same time, independence and the expanded development schemes of the Federation have imposed upon these officers more responsibilities than their British guardians ever had to bear.

Of the second problem facing Malayan bureaucracy as a result of accelerated Malayanization—the imbalance resulting from uneven recruitment—little need be said beyond a brief explanation of the nature of the problem. In many cases middle-aged officers have been quickly pushed to the top by demands of Malayanization and it is here that they will stay for the remainder of their careers. Younger officers, oftentimes inherently more competent, entering the bureaucracy behind clusters of officers only slightly their superiors, cannot look forward to the usual promotions with much optimism in a system where seniority is the primary factor in determining advancement.[26] On the other hand, in later years as these clusters approach retirement, the ranks of the bureaucracy will be decimated in a brief period by the departure of large numbers of senior officers. It was primarily with these long-range difficulties in mind that the first Malayanization Committee made many of its recommendations, arguing that nationalization should proceed only as normal vacancies occurred. For valid political reasons such an approach would have proved impossible, and thus the technical problems the program has produced were in a sense inevitable. Such fatalistic acceptance, however, should not be permitted to obscure the need for future accommodations to relieve some of these pressures. One possibility might be the premature retirement of selected officers, which would remove from the establishment some of the less qualified

26. According to *General Orders*, Cap. A, seniority should not be the primary factor governing promotion. Members of the Public Services Commission and individual officers seem in agreement informally, however, that seniority has become by far the most important qualification. Also see chap. iv, n. 28, below.

bureaucrats and at the same time provide more promising career opportunities for the better qualified younger officers. To the present time, however, the government has shown little interest in such a proposal, and, in fact, in mid-1961 it was announced that the retirement age would be increased across the board by five years.[27]

The third major problem occasioned by the Malayanization scheme is far more difficult to document, though its effects may be observed by witnesses on the scene. As F. S. C. Northrop has so brilliantly pointed out,[28] an element of harmony and consensus-seeking is to be found in all the major cultural areas of Asia. While Northrop limited his observations to China and India, other writers have noted similar characteristics in Japan and Indonesia.[29] It would be tempting to press Northrop's thesis beyond the limits he intended and into the generalization that many of the characteristics he has described as common to Asia are actually one of the characteristics of a traditional as opposed to a modern society. Yet to make such a generalization without benefit of the same painstaking research that Northrop has undertaken would be reckless, and it must therefore be sufficient to point out here that there is considerable evidence to suggest that this desire for consensus and harmony seems also to be present in traditional Malay behavioral patterns. Whether this represents a cultural influence derived from indigenous religious beliefs and practices or a later Indian accretion cannot be stated with certainty, and even tentative conclusions must await more detailed sociological and anthropological research. Nevertheless, such behavior on the

27. See *Straits Budget* (Kuala Lumpur and Singapore), July 26, 1961, p. 14. This proposal was delayed by several months by the opposition of the Staff Side of the Whitley Council but was eventually implemented as originally proposed. The change was undoubtedly necessary since the early retirement age of bureaucrats no longer reflects the life expectancy of Malayans, but had it also been coupled with selected premature retirement (on application or forced) it might have been more palatable to the staff associations and at the same time would have accomplished a dual purpose.

28. *The Meeting of East and West* (New York: The Macmillan Co., 1946), chap. ix.

29. See, for example, Soedjatmoko, "The Role of Political Parties in Indonesia," in Philip W. Thayer, ed., *Nationalism and Progress in Free Asia* (Baltimore: Johns Hopkins Press, 1956), pp. 128–40, esp. 137–38; and Guy J. Pauker, "The Role of the Military in Indonesia," *RAND Corporation Research Memorandum* (Sept., 1960), pp. 48–49. On Japan, see n. 30, below.

part of Malays is observable, and its effect on present-day decision making is equally apparent.[30]

Malay civil servants [31] often exhibit a marked reluctance to do or to say anything that places the individual outside the area of general consensus, for there is always the probability that such a stand will offend an individual or a group who does not share these views. Thus, difficult policy decisions within the bureaucracy are doubly difficult to make. Most Malay officers seem to prefer a compromise that conforms to the general consensus as closely as possible, and if compromise is not possible the alternative next in order of preference is indefinite postponement of the decision until pressures from within or from without force the question.

In the past it was possible to rely upon those outside the Malay cultural environment for the difficult decisions, and the onus for making potentially offensive and non-consensual decisions within the bureaucracy fell upon the expatriate officer. This practice largely continued even after the Malayanization program had replaced the most senior Europeans with indigenous officers. Until the final phase of the Malayanization of the administrative services the general pattern had been to Malayanize the senior-most post of each department while leaving one or several of the immediately subordinate posts in the hands of expatriates. The result was that often it still remained the task of the expatriate, then as the deputy head, to make the difficult policy decisions. Although these were of course made in the name of the department head, it is curious how frequently decisions of this nature were (often correctly) attributed by other indigenous officers not to the locally recruited head but to the lingering influence of the

30. The lingering effects of this quest for conformity have been most carefully analyzed to date in the case of contemporary Japanese politics. Nobutaka Ike, *Japanese Politics: An Introductory Survey* (New York: Knopf, 1957), contains a number of incisive comments about the lingering effect of tradition. Also see Paul S. Dull, "The Political Structure of a Japanese Village," *The Far Eastern Quarterly*, XIII (Feb., 1954), 182–86; and Robert E. Ward, "The Socio-Political Role of the Buraku (Hamlet) in Japan," *American Political Science Review*, XLV (Dec., 1951), 1025–40.

31. My remarks in the remainder of this chapter are confined chiefly to the Malayan Civil Service, since this is the major group responsible for making crucial policy decisions within the bureaucracy.

remaining expatriates.[32] For several years, and to a considerably less extent even now, statistical Malayanization has been more impressive than the actual Malayanization of the decision-making process.

Of course, this reliance on expatriate subordinates must be only of a temporary nature in view of the progress toward total Malayanization, and it will remain for future research to analyze the decision-making process within the completely indigenous bureaucracy. It would be possible to hypothesize at this time that a member of a non-Malay community might take up where the expatriates have left off. As a following chapter will point out, the very nature of the quota system in the MCS has meant that, other things being equal, the average non-Malay in the MCS will be four times better qualified to fill his post than the average Malay. In addition, among members of the non-Malay communities, there would be considerably less tendency to be restrained by the necessity of conforming to the Malay consensus, and thus a correspondingly greater willingness to make the difficult decisions whenever necessary. It therefore seems possible that decision-making responsibilities behind the scenes might increasingly accrue to non-Malay officers, and it seems not unlikely that they may similarly become recognized as the sources of decisions disruptive of the consensus.

32. Added to this cultural factor was the simple historical fact that most of the present-day senior officers served lengthy apprenticeships under expatriate superiors. When the Malayanization program began, these native officers, at the time usually of middle age, were pressed forward by the demands of the scheme into posts for which they were not psychologically prepared, however experienced they might have seemed. Most of these officers had been accustomed to rendering nothing more than routine administrative decisions under the direction of their expatriate superiors, and it is not surprising that in the unfamiliar surroundings of their most senior posts these officers were not reluctant to turn to the more experienced expatriates when difficult problems arose.

4

The Institutional Legacy

Structurally, the public services of the Federation of Malaya are those derived from the British colonial administration, and this bureaucracy itself was a complex machine that had grown around and within the seven diverse but interrelated political entities in the Archipelago. Some colonial servants were assigned directly to the Straits Settlements; some were posted to the Federated Malay States; each of the Unfederated Malay States recruited British officers individually; and all seven units borrowed and lent colonial servants among themselves. Such confused posting as this led to a proliferation of public services that is still one of the striking characteristics of the administrative system. Each of the five formerly Unfederated Malay States has both a state civil service and state clerical services; the four formerly Federated Malay States each has its own state clerical service but no state civil service;[1] and the two present-day states that at one time were part of the Crown Colony of the Straits Settlements have state civil services and distinct clerical establishments, which, unlike the other nine states, do not utilize personnel drawn from the federal clerical services.

Even if discussion is confined to the federal public services,[2] the influence of the historical fragmentation of government is everywhere evident. Except for the "general user services" (the

1. The posts usually filled by the state civil services in the former Unfederated Malay States generally devolve upon personnel of the Malay Administrative Service in the states of the former FMS. On the MAS, see chap. v, below.

2. Since federally appointed officers in Malaya may be assigned to posts that are under the direction of the states, a confusion arises in the term "federal service." By this term I mean those public servants who are recruited by, and whose terms and conditions of service are governed by, the Federal Government, even though many of these officers may be responsible to the individual states in the execution of their duties.

administrative and clerical services), which are not themselves nearly as "general" as the description implies, the public services are structurally fragmented throughout.[3] While the bureaucracy is not unduly large by international comparison, this fragmentation has led to a confusing array of diverse schemes and obscure titles of services.[4] In fact, though it is seldom recognized even by members of the bureaucracy, the whole complex web of federal-state public services is legally held together by a quasi-treaty between the Federal Government, on the one hand, and each of the states individually, on the other.[5]

While the preceding comments probably suggest considerable confusion in the structuring of the bureaucracy as a result of the divergent colonial experience of the constituent units of the present Federation, in fact, on the surface at least, there appears to be remarkable order in the over-all structure. To a great extent this has been accomplished by standardizing salary scales

3. Malayan bureaucracy is structured vertically around the various functional departments, which represents an accidental and pragmatic historical development, and horizontally by design. The horizontal structuring will be discussed in greater detail below.

4. The clerical services have suffered the most chaotic proliferation and fragmentation of services. In the Federation and in the eleven states there were fifty-five different schemes of service for clerical personnel in 1960. Despite a concerted effort on the part of the Federation Establishment Office to reduce this number, there were fifty-three schemes of service in 1962. The problem arises because the scheme of service under which an officer enters into employment is regarded as a contract that binds the government as well as the individual. Thus, unless an officer opts voluntarily to convert to a new scheme, he will remain under his original scheme until he resigns or dies.

5. The original *Malayan Establishment Agreement* was negotiated in 1934 to facilitate transfer of personnel among the various political and administrative units, a subject that is discussed in greater detail below. See Federated Malay States and Singapore, *Malayan Establishment: Agreement, Conditions of Service and Salary Schemes* (Kuala Lumpur: Government Press, n.d.). The last published *Agreement* was dated 1955 and came into effect in 1956. See Federation of Malaya, *Agreement for the Constitution of a Federation Establishment* (Kuala Lumpur: Government Press, 1956). Meeting several weeks before independence, the Conference of Rulers approved certain necessary amendments to the *Agreement* that included the deletion of colonial titles and other such changes. (These amendments were not published but are contained in the Federation Establishment Office in *FEO Conference Series 1180.*) It was provided in these amendments that the appended schedule of posts of the Federation Establishment could be amended on the initiative of the government concerned, with the approval of the Yang di-Pertuan Agong. The last major revision seen by the author was issued on July 1, 1958, and is contained in the unpublished *FEO Series 4910.* Many minor revisions, however, have been made since that time. The Establishment Agreements are difficult to obtain and the two most recent documents have therefore been reprinted below as Appendix B.

and conditions of service and by attempting to persuade many officers in the more obscure services to opt for these revised schemes.

I. The Formal Organization of the Federal Bureaucracy

In addition to a vertical structuring based on the functional departments, there is a horizontal stratification superimposed upon the total bureaucracy consisting of Division I at the top to Division IV at the bottom. Based on a combination of three factors—education, experience, and responsibility—this fourfold stratification grew out of the Trusted Commission *Report* of 1947 and represented a major step in the process of tidying up the bureaucratic structure that had grown without direction over the years.[6] Division I and several Division II services are further structured hierarchically with a broadbase of "timescale" posts above which are a limited number of "superscale" posts, and at the top of the hierarchy are an additional several "staff appointments." Timescale promotions are incremental with only occasional routine examination bars blocking advancement, while the superscale grades "M" through "A" (the top) are pegged to established posts.[7]

To estimate the size of Malayan bureaucracy presents a simple but formidable problem: the last complete count of Malayan governmental employees was made in 1956 and at the present time the Federation Establishment Office is only vaguely aware of the probable size of the bureaucratic machine. Not only is the

6. Malayan Union and Singapore, Public Service Salary Commission of Malaya, 1947 (Sir Harry Trusted, Chairman), *Report* (Kuala Lumpur: Government Press, 1947), *passim*, esp. pp. 6–7.

7. The progression requires some further explanation. For all male officers the grades "A" through "H" are common. There is no superscale "I," and superscale "J", unlike the other superscale posts, carries a fixed salary with an annual increment, characteristic of the timescale. (It was the purpose of this grade to bridge the gap between the top of the non-professional timescale and that of the administrative and professional timescale so that the next step, superscale "H," would be uniform.) The superscale classifications "K," "L," and "M," are women's superscale grades corresponding (at inferior salaries) to the male superscale posts "F," "G," and "H."

1956 census severely dated, but officials privately expressed grave doubts about its accuracy even at the time of its completion. It is for this reason that the statistics gathered here should be viewed with some skepticism at the present time. They are contemporary, and they do represent the most reliable figures available, but these calculations are nevertheless approximations that can stand only until such time as an official census of the bureaucracy is taken.[8] Statistics utilized here have been obtained by tabulating posts enumerated in the Federal *Estimates* and in the *Estimates* of the eleven constituent state governments for the

Table 29. *Federal Bureaucracy, by Division and Ministry*

	Division				
Ministry	I	II	III	IV	Total
Civil List	33	—	—	—	33
Not in ministries	49	64	442	69	624
P. M. Department	152	131	1,390	359	2,032
Agriculture and Co-ops	183	244	940	283	1,650
Commerce and Industry	49	13	175	21	258
Defense	32	15	679	656	1,382
Education	479	167	908	386	1,940
External Affairs	59	37	272	63	431
Treasury	206	255	1,868	430	2,759
Health and Social Welfare	695	609	4,656	10,780	16,740
Interior	91	134	1,301	1,699	3,225
Internal Security	491	1,127	20,077	1,308	23,003
Justice	73	94	461	284	912
Labour	71	108	211	84	474
Rural Development	158	214	1,424	169	1,965
Transport	50	30	463	692	1,235
Works, Posts, Telecomms.	338	311	5,024	1,584	7,257
Totals	3,209	3,553	40,291	18,867	65,920

8. When the Federation Establishment Office in 1960 became aware of this lack of statistical knowledge a crash program was launched to complete a census by mid-1961. Information obtained in the summer of 1962 indicated that this program was not carried through to completion, primarily because of subsequent crash programs of higher priority.

year 1961. While such an approach is far from satisfactory, in Malayan bureaucracy it is necessary.[9]

Table 30. *Total Bureaucracy, by State and Total Federal*

Political Unit	Division				Total
	I	*II*	*III*	*IV*	*Total*
Johore	64	180	613	385	1,242
Kedah	50	157	820	963	1,990
Kelantan	35	79	1,017	286	1,417
Malacca	17	55	283	165	520
Negri Sembilan	40	79	813	428	1,360
Pahang	52	103	1,048	579	1,782
Penang	32	78	410	273	793
Perak	90	163	1,875	1,349	3,477
Perlis	8	20	170	72	270
Selangor	79	141	986	1,042	2,248
Trengganu	29	57	736	291	1,113
State totals	496	1,112	8,771	5,833	16,212
Total Federal Services	3,209	3,553	40,291	18,867	65,920
Total bureaucracy	3,705	4,665	49,062	24,700	82,132

Several relevant generalizations may be derived from tables 29 and 30. (1) By international comparison, Malayan bureaucracy is not unduly large. Allowing for vacancies of 15 per cent, approximately 0.9 per cent of the total population is employed by government in Malaya. While many Malayans view the size of the bureaucratic apparatus with some alarm, this percentage compares not unfavorably with the 1–2 per cent for Latin American countries, 2.2 per cent for Egypt, and 6 per cent for the

9. See Federation of Malaya, *Estimates of Revenue and Expenditure 1st January to 31st December, 1961* (Kuala Lumpur: Government Press, 1961). The most serious deficiency in the Federal *Estimates,* for the purposes of this chapter, is that it is impossible to distinguish between posts that are actually filled and those that are vacant. From available material, it appears that 15 to 20 per cent of all Division I posts are vacant at the present time, but it is impossible even to estimate the number of vacancies in the lower divisions. A second disadvantage that is less serious is that it is possible to distinguish between Federal and state employees only on the basis of who pays the salaries, not on the more logical basis of which unit recruits the officers.

United Kingdom,[10] and is not greatly out of line with the 0.3–0.5 per cent figure for Pakistan.[11]

(2) Of interest to students of Malayan federalism, it should be noted that the Federal Government is by far the largest single employer of bureaucrats in Malaya, and in fact it alone employs more than four times as many monthly-salaried employees as the eleven state governments combined. Even this figure, however, is not an accurate quantification of federal-state bureaucratic relations, for it must be remembered that a high percentage of the Division I posts shown on the state tabulations are officers whose salaries are paid from state funds but whose terms and conditions of service are established by the Federal Government and who have been recruited by the Federal Government.[12]

(3) Statistical tabulation proves that it is at the level of Division III that Malayan bureaucracy is largest, and personal observation suggests that it is here that the rational bureaucratic apparatus is weakest. The Trusted Commission *Report* recommended that Division III should be composed, among others, of technical assistants, religious and vernacular teachers not in the regular stream of national education, and the bulk of the clerical services. The normal educational level would probably be completion, or near completion, of secondary school, sometimes in the vernacular stream and in many cases from the English stream of education.[13] Due to the demands of the Malayanization program the

10. See Joseph J. Spengler, "Public Bureaucracy, Resource Structure, and Economic Development; A Note," *Kyklos*, XI (1958), 479.
11. Correspondence with Professor Ralph Braibanti of Duke University, then Adviser to the Civil Service Academy, Lahore, Pakistan. Professor Braibanti's figures exclude posts and telegraphs, which have been included in the tabulations of the preceding pages. Using the population projection for 1962 ("Medium" fertility), the population of Malaya was about 7.46 million. See Federation of Malaya, *1957 Population Census, Report No. 14* (Kuala Lumpur: Department of Statistics, 1962), Table 7.14B.
12. The question of jurisdictional responsibility over these officers in matters of discipline has never been pressed to its conclusion. There is no doubt that they are subject to the Federal Public Services Commission, but some state officials have put forward the logical argument that in the execution of their duties they are subject to the control of the state, and hence under the jurisdiction of the state public service commissions. Despite often repeated denials by federal officials, it seems probable that a jurisdictional clash will eventually arise though the traditional urge to avoid such confrontations of extremes may postpone it until a crucial issue forces the question.
13. See n. 6, above.

best qualified of these Division III officers have now moved into Division II (and in some cases into Division I) to replace those who were promoted to the senior bureaucracy to replace the departing expatriates. Thus, by original intent now reinforced by accident, Division III is staffed primarily by a group in whom the often conflicting behavioral demands of modernity and tradition within the individual personality are most marked, and, at the same time, it is at this level of government that the "modern" civil servant must come to grips with many situations of a more "traditional" nature. After lengthy investigations of alleged corruption in the public services, the Taylor Commission in 1955 found the bureaucracy as a whole to be remarkably free of suspicion, but it also concluded:

> We believe that bribery and other forms of corruption are practised in all *vulnerable* departments but there is no evidence from which either the actual or the comparative incidence can be estimated. . . . *The most vulnerable departments are those . . . which necessarily have large numbers of the lower ranks in direct contact with the public* in circumstances where both are tempted and supervision is difficult and remote. . . .[14]

Bureaucratic corruption at this level is always a problem, but in a social environment where "tea money" is an accepted means of getting something done, the probability of such practices is considerably increased. And, as the preceding tables demonstrate, it is at this vulnerable level that the broad base of the bureaucracy is to be found.

Salaries and perquisites of present-day government officers also reflect the transitional nature of Malayan bureaucracy. As a general rule salaries of Division I officers are superior to those of posts in private industry filled by Malayans of approximately the same ages and possessing similar educational qualifications and experience. During the colonial period salaries of senior bureaucrats had to be competitive with those of commercial expatriates

14. Federation of Malaya, *Report of the Commission to Enquire into Matters Affecting the Integrity of the Public Services, 1955* (Kuala Lumpur: Government Press, 1955), p. 59 (emphasis added). The *Report* as a whole was accepted as reliable, but Government issued a stinging rebuttal to a number of the sharp personal criticisms of departmental personnel (which it then included as an insert in the official *Report*).

and were therefore pegged to a very comfortable British standard of living. At the same time local conditions have largely determined the salary scales of the less senior posts. The result is that at the present time there is great disparity between the average salaries of junior and senior bureaucrats.[15]

The differential indicated in the salary scales does not, moreover, reflect the true picture of the difference in real income. To the basic salary is added a Cost of Living Allowance that varies according to the salary of the bureaucrat, the size of the family, etc. Public servants are provided either with subsidized housing, for which only token rental is paid, or, when housing is not available, with a graduated housing allowance based on the type of quarters for which the servant, by virtue of his grade, would otherwise be eligible. Medical care for government officers is provided almost free of charge in government medical facilities; leave regulations are extremely liberal; and a number of miscellaneous benefits have accrued such as interest-free auto loans without cash payment for senior officers, clothing allowances for regular duty in the temperate zones, and other minor leave, educational, and travel benefits. Of course, officers on the permanent establishment also participate in a pension scheme. Although several of the benefits favor the lower grades on a proportional basis, on the whole the perquisites of governmental service in Malaya tend to increase rather than decrease the economic and social distance that separates the officers of Division I from those of Divisions II–IV.

The origins of the major benefits attached to service in the senior bureaucracy can be traced directly to the nature of the public services in the colonial period. The senior bureaucracy was geared to the needs of the expatriate officers, and the added benefits were a necessary inducement to attract men to a country where housing, medical facilities, and transportation were inferior to those enjoyed in England. As a result the government found

15. The maximum salary listed in the present *Staff List* is $756.67 per month; the lowest salary listed in the *Schemes of Service* is $15.83 per month. This of course represents the maximum differential. Division I ranges from approximately $185 to $756.57; Division II, $100–$270; Division III, $35–$200; and Division IV, $16–$65.

it necessary to provide free medical service of high quality, government quarters or housing subsidies to compensate for the high cost of Western-style rentals on the open market, and motorcycles or automobiles to assist the officers in moving around their districts. With independence and the Malayanization of most of the bureaucracy these benefits have passed on almost intact to the incoming indigenous officers. While the original logic for the perquisites might not be open to question, such luxuries as the once per lifetime round-trip passage (with voyage leave) seems markedly outdated when it is used by Malayan officers for the purposes of going "home" (England). However, it seems unlikely that benefits such as these will disappear easily so long as the present period of political and economic stability continues.[16]

II. Internal Administration of the Bureaucracy

In general, the organs charged with the internal administration of the bureaucracy, as the bureaucracy as a whole, represent an attempt to implant British ideas and institutions on Malayan soil

16. The Atkinson Housing Proposals offer some evidence of the difficulties involved in abolishing a well established benefit. The basic principle underlying the Proposals was that officers residing in the general area where they are posted should not be provided with government quarters, but should be assisted in owning their own homes. In effect, this represented a compromise that it was hoped would help the government to get out from under its continuing housing responsibilities, but even such a compromise, which is certainly liberal by most standards, has thus far not proved acceptable. Originally submitted in 1952, the Atkinson Proposals are still under consideration in the National Whitley Council. See Federation of Malaya, G. A. Atkinson, *Report on the Housing for Division I Government Officers in the Federation of Malaya* (Kuala Lumpur: Government Press, 1952), and *Report on Housing for Government Officers in Division II and Lower Divisions, the Federation of Malaya* (Kuala Lumpur: Government Press, 1953). For a summary of the progress of the Proposals before the Whitley Council, see Federation of Malaya, National Whitley Council (Divisions I–IV), Staff Side, *Eighth Annual Report* (Kuala Lumpur: Loyal Press, 1961), pp. 8–9. The Proposals thus far have probably been defeated by an almost unconscious coalition of the senior and junior bureaucracy who have been pursuing an identical goal for sometimes different reasons. It appears that the subordinate bureaucracy is motivated chiefly by middle-class conservatism, a desire to keep what they have and not to take a chance on something that is untried. To a certain extent this probably also enters into the thinking of senior bureaucrats, but a number of the more senior officers also have economic motives, since many own one or more houses that are leased out at economic rents while they in turn are living in government or government-subsidized quarters. From cursory observation it seems that this practice is limited chiefly to senior officers resident in the federal capital where Western-style housing is in great demand at generally inflated rentals.

in the hope that the seeds will take root and that the product will generally resemble the original as closely as possible. Borrowed complete with British terminology, the major organs concerned are the Federation Establishment Office, the public service commissions, and the Whitley councils.

The FEO grew out of the original Malayan Establishment Office created under the terms of the Malayan Establishment Agreement of 1934 [17] to bring some order from the chaos of lending and borrowing that had developed throughout the Peninsula. The MEO continued in existence until 1954, but with the growing separation of Singapore and Malaya, which was formalized in the Malayan Union scheme and continued under the Federation Agreement of 1948, a single establishment was becoming more and more a fiction. In practice two separate and distinct establishment offices were growing up, a trend that finally was given formal recognition by the separation of the two offices in the Agreement of 1954.[18] The creation of the FEO, as it still exists today, actually represented an amalgamation of three units that had been in existence for some time. Brought together in 1954 were the Service Branch of the Chief Secretary's Office (created in 1946), the Federation section of the MEO, and the Establishments Division of the Treasury.[19]

The precise relationship between the FEO and the public service commissions is not easy to define. In general, the Public Services Commission (the major public service commission) is responsible for all initial appointments, promotions, confirmations, and—with certain exceptions—disciplinary matters. In some cases the departments concerned deal directly with the PSC, but in all matters concerning the general user services (primarily the administrative and clerical services) the FEO acts as

17. See n. 5, above.
18. See Federation of Malaya, *Agreement for the Constitution of a Federation Establishment* (Kuala Lumpur: Government Press, 1956). Although the FEO was created in 1954 at the time that the Agreement was signed, the document was not ratified by all of the states until 1956.
19. See Federation of Malaya, *General Circular No. 7 of 1954,* "The Federation Establishment Office" (Kuala Lumpur: Government Press, 1954). The Establishments Division of the Treasury was created in 1952 by dividing the functions of the Service Branch of the Chief Secretary's Office. See Federation of Malaya, *Service Circular No. 22 of 1951,* "The Establishments Division" (Kuala Lumpur: Government Press, 1951).

a clearing house to supply information to the PSC. In addition, the Principal Establishment Officer prepares confidential service reports and countersigns recommendations of supervisors in cases where the officer concerned is a member of a "common user service," on the rationale that the PEO is technically the department head. The FEO is responsible for conducting training courses to be attended by public servants within the country, but in most cases the PSC is responsible for selecting the officers who will attend these courses. It seems that many of the functions now exercised by the PSC were held first by the Service Branch of the Chief Secretary's Office and then by the FEO. Between 1954 and 1960 the tendency was to pass more and more duties to the PSC, but since 1960 it is possible that this trend has been reversed.

During the colonial period of Malayan administration the responsibilities usually associated with the present PSC either were delegated to the various department heads or—in the case of overseas recruitment—left in the hands of the Colonial Office or the Crown Agents for the colonies. Recruitment of local personnel was undertaken either in the name of the Chief Secretary or by departmental selection boards composed of senior government officers. In overseas recruitment, the source of almost all of the senior personnel, machinery was set up in the United Kingdom by the Secretary of State for the Colonies. The promotion of lower grade servants, like local recruitment, was generally left to the discretion of department heads, usually acting on the advice of departmental promotion boards. For senior personnel, after 1934, recommendations for promotion emanated from a special board constituted within the Malayan Establishment Office, and after 1952 all Division I recruitment and promotion had to receive the approval of the High Commissioner. Disciplinary matters were usually the responsibility of the departments, except that the final authority where senior officers were concerned was the Secretary of State for the Colonies.

A Colonial Office White Paper of 1946 introduced a new era in the internal administration of the colonial bureaucracy. According to the new official policy, "the future of each Colony rests ultimately in the hands of its own people," and thus machinery should be introduced that would foster the development of local responsibility. One piece of machinery was to be the public service commissions:

Public Service Commissions should be established in the Colonies. Subject to the general overriding powers of the Secretary of State, the selection and appointment of candidates in the Colonies to posts in the local service will lie with the Governor of the Colony. It is desirable that the Governor should be advised in these matters by a Public Service Commission appointed by him and so composed as to command the confidence of the Service and Public.[20]

Originally, in Malaya, it was intended that the public service commission recommended in Colonial No. 197 should be a statutory body drawing its legal existence from an act passed by the Federal Legislative Council, and a motion to this effect was introduced by a Malayan member in 1948.[21] However, with the almost immediate upheaval caused by the Emergency, further consideration was deferred until 1953, when a committee was appointed to reopen investigations of the question. The Committee's *Report*, laid before the Council in March, 1954,[22] recommended the introduction of an act to create a public service commission and announced the decision of Government to create a temporary Public Service Appointments and Promotions Board that would function until such time as the statutory commission came into existence. Although the Government somewhat belatedly introduced such legislation in the Council in June, 1955, the sudden nationalistic opposition the bill encountered caused the British administrators to withdraw the act quickly and take a sober second look at the need for a public service commission.[23]

20. Great Britain, Colonial Office, *Organization of the Colonial Service* (London: HMSO, 1946) [Col. No. 197 of 1946], pp. 4–5, 9.

21. Federation of Malaya, Legislative Council (First Session), *Proceedings* (Kuala Lumpur: Government Press, 1951), pp. B74–78.

22. Federation of Malaya, Legislative Council (Seventh Session), *Minutes and Council Papers* (Kuala Lumpur: Government Press, 1954), Paper No. 9 of 1954, "Establishment of a Public Service Commission."

23. The major criticism of the bill was that it excluded from the jurisdiction of the proposed commission many senior posts, which was interpreted as certain evidence that the British intended to delay the Malayanization of these posts as long as possible. The speech by one member (Inche Mohamed Rashid) is revealing of this attitude:

"The intention behind the proposed creation of the Public Service Commission —at least my own intention—is solely and primarily for the purpose of establish-

As a result the supposedly temporary Public Service Appointments and Promotions Board was again given added life.

When the proposal for a public service commission next appeared it took the form of a body not grounded in federal law but actually included as an integral part of the Federation Constitution.[24] This London Conference proposal was accepted and three Commissions (Designate)—as the Public Services Commission, the Judicial Service Commission, and the Police Service Commission were officially known—began operation on January 1, 1957.[25] With Merdeka and the promulgation of the present Constitution on August 31, 1957, the qualifier "designate" was dropped and the Federation finally had a full-fledged system of public service commissions.[26]

The composition and the terms of service of the chairmen and the members are spelled out in detail in the Constitution. In the Public Services Commission, either or both the chairman and the deputy chairman must have been public servants within a five-year period preceding their first appointments, and both of these,

---

ing and accelerating the Malayanization of the Government service in the country . . . , and all of us are in favor of Malayanization in the shortest possible time." (Federation of Malaya, Legislative Council [Eighth Session], *Proceedings* [Kuala Lumpur: Government Press, 1956], pp. B573, B680–90.)

In view of the recommendations of the first *Malayanization Report* (1954) these criticisms probably had some validity, though it might be questioned here whether the member meant Malayanization or Malay-ization.

24. See Federation of Malaya, Second Legislative Council (First Session), *Minutes and Council Papers* (Kuala Lumpur: Government Press, 1957), Paper No. 6 of 1956, "Report of the Federation of Malaya Constitutional Conference Held in London in January and February 1956."

25. As the Constitution finally emerged, there were provisions for four commissions—the three listed above under slightly different titles plus a Railway Service Commission. By a constitutional amendment of 1960 the Judicial and Legal Service Commission was abolished and its functions were transferred chiefly to the Public Services Commission. At the same time the Police Service Commission became the Police Forces Commission and was reconstituted similar to the Armed Forces Council, which is also a constitutional body. The principle of bureaucratic neutrality is given a legal basis in the Constitutional instrument. The relevant section (Part X), which provides a surprisingly detailed outline of the institutions of bureaucracy, is reprinted below as Appendix C.

26. This is speaking in formal terms, of course. In fact, the guiding personnel of the bodies changed little from the time of the Public Service Appointments and Promotions Board onward, and while the PSAPB was purely advisory, its advice was so seldom questioned that it actually differed little from the later constitutional body. The Reports of the PSAPB were not published but are available in Kuala Lumpur in typescript (*Report for the Period June to December 1954*) and mimeograph (*Report for the Year 1955 and Report for the Year Ending 31st December 1956*).

plus the four to eight other members, are appointed for five-year terms by the Yang di-Pertuan Agong acting on the advice of his Prime Minister. There is interlocking membership between the Public Services Commission and the Railway Service Commission, and the members of all commissions can be removed only through the elaborate procedures established for the removal of a judge of the Supreme Court.[27]

The work of the Public Services Commission has been distinguished though perhaps somewhat unimaginative. Recruitment figures set out in Chapter III indicate that, at least in the senior services, the Commission has apparently not been greatly influenced by communal pressures. The Chinese and Indians have been recruited to the senior bureaucracy in relatively larger numbers than have the Malays, and there is little positive evidence to suggest that the PSC has often succumbed to outside influence even in specific individual cases. The question of discipline and promotion is more difficult to assess since it is not possible to tabulate and quantify the results of the Commission's work. However, even a cursory examination of the annual *Staff Lists* will confirm the allegations made by many government officers that Malayan bureaucracy is more a gerontocracy than a merit system. Although the *General Orders* states that "officers will be selected for promotion on the basis of official qualifications, experience and merit [and] only where two candidates are adjudged of equal merit will preference be given to the senior," [28] in fact it is rare in the senior bureaucracy that an officer outside the "promotion zone" is jumped over the heads of his colleagues. There may be isolated cases of promotions based on ascriptive

27. This procedure is also spelled out in the Constitution. The Yang di-Pertuan Agong must receive a recommendation for such removal from an *ad hoc* tribunal presided over by the Chief Justice and composed of at least five judges or former judges of the Supreme Court (or persons with equivalent qualifications from any Commonwealth country).

28. Cap. A. para. 38. On one occasion the author borrowed from a senior member of the Public Services Commission a copy of the scarce volume, C. J. Hayes, *Report of the Public Service Commissions of British Commonwealth Countries* (London: Civil Service Commission, 1955). At one point Mr. Hayes commented that while the basis of promotion throughout the Commonwealth was merit, it was usually safest in the long run to rely upon the more objective standard of seniority. It seems more than a coincidence that this page was well worn and that the particular passage was underscored and starred.

factors other than longevity, but in the senior bureaucracy, where the *Staff Lists* provide a reasonably reliable guide, these cases seem statistically insignificant unless they are indicative of new trends.

Unlike Pakistan, where the Writ Petition has become a popular means of seeking redress for alleged administrative wrongs,[29] the judicial avenues of appeal in Malaya have not been well traveled. In fact, only a single case appealing an administrative ruling has found its way to the ultimate court of appeal, the Privy Council of the British Crown, and the substance of this case is of considerably diminished importance since the constitutional amendments of 1960, while a second and more relevant case went only so far as the High Court.[30] However, the mere fact that the courts have expressed a willingness, albeit somewhat hesitantly, to look into the administrative decisions of the service commissions indicates that the precedents have now been established which will be enlarged upon by practice in the future.

While, on the whole, the PSC has observed admirable objectivity in recruitment to the senior bureaucracy, together with the FEO, it has in another sense served as the instrument for maintaining *de facto* Malay supremacy. Recruitment quotas, sanctioned by the Constitution, fix the recruitment ratios in a number of the key services to the distinct disadvantage of the non-Malay communities.[31] It is the responsibility of the FEO to serve

29. See Ralph Braibanti, "Bureaucracy and Judiciary in Pakistan," in Joseph LaPalombara, ed., *Bureaucracy and Political Development* (Princeton: Princeton University Press, 1963), pp. 418–34.

30. The Surinder Singh Kanda case involved a Police Inspector dismissed from his post by the then Commissioner of Police. The case, which was eventually decided by the Privy Council, turned on a question of Constitutional interpretation and dealt only indirectly with judicial oversight of administrative decisions. The more relevant case was *Rashia Munusamy v. The Public Services Commission* (High Court of Kuala Lumpur, unpublished). Although the High Court upheld the Commission, *obiter dicta* suggested that the Court felt itself competent to review the Commission's decisions when it was called upon to do so. However, even here the Court hedged and based its reasoning on the fact that certain disciplinary procedures of the Commission are included in the Constitution and thus "any action by the Commission in contravention . . . [of these] must be constitutionally invalid."

31. The Constitution (Article 153 [2]) provides that the "Yang di-Pertuan Agong shall . . . safeguard the special position of the Malays and . . . ensure the reservation for Malays of such proportion as he may deem reasonable of positions in the public service. . . ." Furthermore, by paragraph 3, to carry out this duty the Yang di-Pertuan Agong may "give such general directions as may be

as the watchdog to guarantee the observance of the quotas, and it is the duty of the PSC to recruit on a dual standard so as to carry out the instructions of the FEO. Thus, in this sense the PSC does not aspire for complete objectivity. However, in fairness it must be pointed out that neither the PSC nor the FEO has any choice in the matter, and if the dual standard of recruitment is to be criticized (which it often is, inside as well as outside Malaya), then the criticism should be directed at a considerably higher level where the idea of a quota system originated and is maintained.

The third major segment concerned with the internal administration of the bureaucracy is the Whitley Council machinery. The idea of Whitleyism,[32] with its closed deliberations and compromise consensus, struck a sympathetic chord in Malaya and the institutions of Whitleyism proliferated. While the earliest attempts to implement Whitley machinery in Malaya had been unsuccessful primarily for technical reasons,[33] the institutional arrangements left behind by W. J. Haimes in 1953 [34] today form the basis for employer-employee communications and negotiations in the government services. There are now two National Whitley Councils (Divisions I–IV and Daily Rated), a Police Council, a National Joint Council of Teachers, and a large number of departmental Whitley Councils. The formal organization

---

required . . . to any [public service] Commission . . . and the Commission . . . shall duly comply with the directions." It is on this Constitutional basis that a recruitment quota of four Malays to each non-Malay has been established for the Malayan Civil Service and 3:1 for the External Affairs Service. In addition, quotas are applied to parts of several other services, to scholarships, bursaries, and training awards.

32. Whitleyism in Britain grew out of the *Report* of a committee under the chairmanship of J. H. Whitley appointed to investigate means of improving employer-employee relations in industry. See Great Britain, *Accounts and Papers, 1917–1918*, Vol. 18, Cmd. 8606, "Interim Report on Joint Standing Industrial Councils." In 1919, under pressure from staff associations, Whitleyism was adopted by the public services, with "labor" and "management" becoming the "Staff Side" and the "Official Side."

33. In the earlier period, and to a lesser extent today, the superstructure of Whitleyism was built without any foundations. It was impossible to select a Staff Side due to the highly segmented nature of the staff associations. It has been estimated that in 1951 there were no less than 130 registered staff unions, many having only the minimum of seven members required for registration as a union.

34. Even today the Haimes *Report* remains the handbook that guides Malayan Whitleyism. See W. J. Haimes, *Report to His Excellency the Officer Administering the Government, Sir Donald MacGillivray* (Kuala Lumpur: mimeographed, 1953).

of Malayan Whitleyism is indeed impressive, but the functioning of the system is at least revealing and sometimes sobering. The National Whitley Council (Divisions I–IV) is by far the most important of the institutions of Whitleyism, and its organization, strengths, and weaknesses are also typical of each of the other organs of consultation. Thus, the major examples of Malayan Whitleyism will be based on the experience of this body.

Following the model of British Whitleyism, even to the use of the terminology, the National Whitley Council is composed of an Official Side of nineteen members, appointed by the Yang di-Pertuan Agong, and a Staff Side of twenty-two, selected by groups of staff associations and public service unions.[35] The Chairman of the National Whitley Council is constitutionally the Chairman of the Official Side, a post that throughout its history has been filled by the most senior government officer in Malaya, since independence the Permanent Secretary, Prime Minister's Department. When functioning smoothly, which in recent years has been more the exception than the rule, much of the business of the Whitley Council is carried on informally, often between the two most active principals, the secretaries of the two sides. When not functioning smoothly, Whitley negotiations have either been suspended completely, or the two sides have been able to find little or no area of agreement.[36]

On the whole, Whitleyism has had a frustrating history in Malaya thus far. After the initial false start, it seemed that the Whitley idea had quickly taken root as a result of the seeds sown

35. The bulk of these members (twelve) are selected by CUEPACS, the Congress of Unions of Employees in the Public and Civil Services. Also represented are the European Civil Servants Association of Malaya, the Malayan Civil Service Association, the Senior Government Officers Association, and the Malay Administrative Service Association. CUEPACS emerged in September, 1958, as an attempt to draw together in a loose federation the highly segmented public service union movement. Its growth, while not spectacular, has been steady and it now constitutes the dominant voice of the unions representing the less senior services.

36. Reference is made here, of course, to major issues before the Council. Minor issues, such as the issuance of a new *General Order*, have often been approved by the Joint Council—that is, the full membership of 41, which sits only once a year to ratify the decisions of the General Purposes Committee and the Combined Grades Committee. The Staff Side issues annual reports, each, since the *Second Annual Report*, published privately in Kuala Lumpur. (The first report was unpublished.) The annual reports of the Joint Council are titled *Bulletins* and have been published annually by the Federation Establishment Office since 1954.

by W. J. Haimes. But thus far the Whitley machinery has failed to function precisely as Mr. Haimes presupposed that it would in 1953. All of the major conflicts and contradictions to be found throughout Malayan society manifest themselves in the practice of Malayan Whitleyism. The differing attitudes of the three major communities toward labor organization is revealed by the disproportionate number of Indians who are active in Staff Side activities.[37] Within the Council the stresses and strains of the rapid transition into the era of modernity are apparent in the individuals who make up the working bodies. Whitleyism brings together the two categories of public servants that are most widely separated on the traditional-modern spectrum, and they must come together not as subordinates and superiors but as equals.[38] Yet the Official Side often behaves as if it is *primus inter pares*, steadfastly refusing to consider a request which Government may feel (often with good reason) to be beyond the jurisdiction of the Whitley Council. To many members of the Staff Side and its supporting associations, such a dogmatic stand not only violates the principles of Whitleyism as they understand it, but it also goes against the more fundamental principle of seeking a compromise consensus and compels each party to take an either-or position, a stand from which one side must eventually withdraw with a resulting loss of face. Added to these frustrations is the fact that the Staff Side itself has undergone a functional mutation in the Malayan

37. Though comprising probably no more than 15–20 per cent of the total bureaucracy, Indians accounted for almost one-half the delegates to the First Annual Convention of CUEPACS held in late 1959. Of 51 delegates, only seven were Chinese. See CUEPACS, *Annual Report and Statement of Accounts, 1959–60* (Kuala Lumpur: The Economy Printers, Ltd., 1960), pp. 5–6. Labor leaders often confess in private that recruitment among the Chinese is exceedingly difficult.

38. There is some evidence that at the departmental level this may serve a communications function that did not exist before the adoption of Whitleyism. In a detailed examination of a single departmental Whitley Council the Secretary of the Staff Side, a Division III officer, pointed out to the author that in Malaya a great social chasm separates officers of Division I from those of Divisions II–IV. Prior to the creation of his departmental Whitley Council there was little possibility of communication between the two groups even within the department. However, since the Chairman of the Council (the Deputy Director of the Department) and the other members of the Official Side are all senior officers, there is now the opportunity for the two groups to discuss matters of mutual interest without the debilitations caused by differing statuses. The Secretary was speaking more in terms of general departmental business than about matters of a more specifically Whitley nature, another indication that the functional role of Whitley machinery has undergone some mutations in the changed environment of Malaya.

environment that makes it doubly difficult to fulfil its role in the Whitley system. On several occasions the Staff Side, rather than negotiating quietly behind the scenes, has served as the instrument for aggregating public political interests and then articulating these in no uncertain manner through the English language press. On at least one occasion this operation was highly effective,[39] but it was probably not one of the functions of Malayan Whitleyism that Haimes would have predicted in 1953.

In summary, the bureaucratic structure of contemporary Malaya is a replica of the system left behind by the departing British —the colonial model with only a minimum of structural modifications. Yet, while the structures have remained remarkably similar to those of the colonial period, the functions that these perform within the total political and social system are beginning to show evidences of becoming peculiarly Malayan. Functional mutations of existing structures—most evident in the Whitley machinery but also becoming apparent in other institutions—make the offspring behave somewhat differently from the parent. Having said this, however, it should not be implied that the efficiency of the Malayan bureaucratic machine has been considerably diminished. On the contrary, Malaya's bureaucratic efficiency cannot be

---

39. In April, 1960, the Government introduced into Parliament, among other Constitutional amendments, certain changes that affected the working of the Public Services Commission. Meeting almost immediately following the introduction of the amendments, the Staff Side of the General Purposes Committee demanded that the bills should be submitted for the consideration of the Whitley Council before being introduced to Parliament. The Official Side replied that it was a matter of government policy and not a proper matter for Whitley Council consideration. At this point the Staff Side walked out and called Whitley discussions to a halt in symbolic protest, announcing their decision in a well timed press conference that received considerable attention in the English-language press. When debate began on the proposed amendments two days later opposition members frequently cited the action of the Staff Side as clear evidence of popular disapproval. With the overwhelming majority enjoyed by the Alliance in Parliament there was never any serious doubt that the amendments would be approved if put to a vote. However, it is probable that the adverse publicity the amendments received, due in no small part to the action of the Staff Side, was responsible for the Government's decision to delete several of the most objectionable features of some of the amendments. Moreover, while the PSC amendment was passed much as it was originally framed, it seems significant that the Government has come to interpret it as an "enabling act" and as yet the proposed changes have not been implemented, a compromise that is itself suggestive of the nature of Malayan politics. For contemporary newspaper accounts, see *Sunday Mail* (Kuala Lumpur) and *Sunday Times* (Singapore and Kuala Lumpur), April 17, 1960; *Straits Times* (Singapore and Kuala Lumpur), April 19, 21, and 23, 1960, and *Malay Mail* (Kuala Lumpur) for the same dates.

doubted, for even on a standard of measurement based on the colonial bureaucracy itself the accomplishments of independent Malaya's bureaucracy have indeed been impressive.

Throughout this chapter little has been said about two related subjects of crucial importance to the course of political change in Malaya. The emphasis has been on the technical and professional bureaucracy while little attention has been paid to the administrative services and to their role in the conduct of Malayan government. It is clearly evident that Malayan bureaucracy has been admirably successful in securing for the country the fruits of economic prosperity, and here credit must be given to all components of the senior bureaucracy. But health of the polity cannot be judged purely on material standards, and when questions are raised about bureaucracy and the political process it becomes necessary to focus specifically on the dynamic nucleus of Malayan bureaucracy—the Malayan Civil Service.

5

The Administrative Legacy

During the colonial period in Malaya the administrative services—primarily the Malayan Civil Service—constituted the predominant voice in the day-to-day control of affairs of government. The decisions of MCS officers, particularly those in the field, were likely to be highly discretionary; and MCS personnel had a hand in policy formulation on the federal level.[1] Thus, the senior administrative service was often involved in decision-making that was sometimes as political as it was administrative, and this dominant position of the MCS in the political process elevated the Service and its members to a unique status comparable to that of the ICS in India.

I. The Position of the MCS in the Bureaucratic Hierarchy

The importance of the present-day MCS is clearly evidenced by observing the internal structuring of the services, by noting the key posts that MCS officers fill in government, and by considering even in a cursory manner the diverse and important tasks that MCS officers are called upon to perform.

A comparison of the grade structure of the bureaucracy, presented graphically on page 103, is adequate to demonstrate the

1. MCS officers constituted a large and important part of the Federal Legislative Council, where, in 1937 for example, they accounted for almost one-half the total membership. These included, among other MCS members, the four Residents, the Federal Secretary, Legal Adviser, Financial Adviser, Adviser on Education, Commissioner of Customs and Excise, Controller of Labour, and Secretary for Chinese Affairs. See Federated Malay States, *Proceedings of the Federal Council, 1937* (Kuala Lumpur: Government Press, 1938).

attractiveness of a career in the MCS, leaving aside for the moment all other considerations of relative power and prestige. For the young officer entering the Division I bureaucracy, the prospects for promotion to a superscale post are nowhere as bright as they are in the MCS. In fact, from the point of view of pure statistical probability, it appears that in the non-MCS bureaucracy the possibility of many career officers retiring from the top of the timescale cannot be ruled out under normal circumstances; yet in the MCS it seems unlikely that any career officer who entered at the normal age of recruitment would fail to rise at least to the first superscale rung by the time of his retirement. Thus, if an opening is available, the MCS is the logical choice of any young aspiring bureaucrat with the requisite educational and ascriptive qualifications.

Graph 2. *Structure of Selected Division I Services*

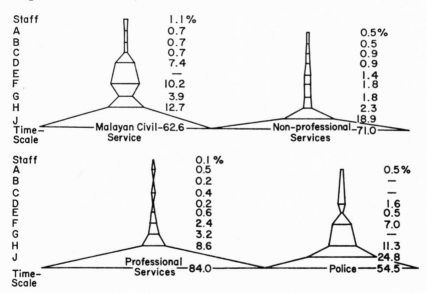

While other Division I services are confined largely to individual ministries, or at most to several ministries, officers of the MCS are to be found assigned to key positions in every ministry except one. In addition to a number of other key posts, senior MCS personnel hold positions as Permanent Secretaries (or Secretaries as they are still termed in a number of ministries) throughout government with the single exception of the Ministry of External Affairs; MCS officers staff the State Secretaryships in six of the states of the Federation; and they serve as Commissioners of Lands and Mines in eight states. Moreover, in all of their assignments, it is the exception rather than the rule for the senior MCS officer of a ministry to be subordinate in rank and salary to the senior professional officer of the ministry.

Not only are MCS officers to be found in policy-making slots in the federal capital, but historically the influence of the Service has always covered the length and breadth of the Peninsula. Administrative officers of the MCS are posted to every state of the Federation, and many of these are located in field posts where they provide a major contact between the government and the governed.[2]

A cursory observation of the institutional structure alone is adequate to demonstrate the dominant position enjoyed by the MCS in the total bureaucratic structure. The grade structure, the pan-governmental nature of MCS assignments, and the broad geographic distribution of members of the senior administrative service attest to its elevated importance in the Malayan bureaucratic system. Moreover, the MCS can claim direct descent from the most famous of all modern administrative services, and this relation to the ICS is itself productive of certain prestige that the contemporary MCS still enjoys.

II. The MCS and the ICS: Continuity and Discontinuity

The historical indebtedness of the MCS to the ICS has been traced in an earlier chapter,[3] and it remains here only to point

2. In 1962 ninety-eight timescale officers were serving in ten of the eleven states of the Federation (the single exception being Kelantan, where such assignments were usually filled by members of the Kelantan Civil Service. The Commissioner of Lands and Mines is, however, an MCS post in Kelantan.)

3. See chap. iii, above, pp. 45 ff.

out several of the salient characteristics of the ICS that have been passed on almost intact to the MCS or that have undergone alteration in the Malayan setting. Basic to both services is the concept of an administrative generalist, conceived of as a man capable of being an "administrator" regardless of the nature of the functional group to which he is posted. Thus, in theory, an MCS officer should at first serve a number of years in district administration, ideally serving in many different areas before he is finally brought in to staff a position in the federal capital. While this was the common pattern of the pre-independence MCS, the increasing demand for a scarce commodity and the growing complexity of government have combined often to make theory and practice fail to coincide, a fact that has grudgingly received some official attention.[4] Yet, to an extent far greater than can be found in American practice, administrative officers by educational qualifications and by experience are still generalists. Only two avenues of recruitment into the MCS are open, and both of these virtually assure the continuation of the administrative generalist spirit for the foreseeable future. Personnel entering through a junior administrative service will probably already have this spirit inculcated in their own outlooks, and those recruited directly from the universities with a B.A. (Honors) have an educational background that is conducive to creating the same attitudes.[5] The desirability of the generalist approach in the administrative bureaucracy is seldom seriously questioned in Malaya, and deviations from this norm are usually dismissed as exigencies caused by the demands of the transitional period. This belief might well be defended on rational grounds, although in the Federation the sanctity of past practice is usually invoked to put an end to all discussions of the advantages or disadvantages of the administrative generalist approach.

4. Federation of Malaya, *General Circular No. 4 of 1959,* "Organization within Ministries" (Kuala Lumpur: Government Press, 1959), par. 20, recognized that in some of the more specialized ministries it was probable that an MCS officer would advance vertically, possibly without being transferred horizontally to another ministry throughout his career.

5. At the present time, 169 MCS officers have been promoted from the junior administrative services; 88 have been recruited directly from universities. The topic is discussed in more detail in a later section.

Examination charisma, another salient characteristic of the ICS tradition, has not fared as well in the Malayan environment as has the faith in administrative generalists, though traces of it are still to be found at somewhat different levels in the administrative bureaucracy. As noted in a previous chapter,[6] the qualification examination for entry into the MCS did not survive the unification of the colonial services in 1932. Thus, the magic of the open competitive examination, still so evident in recruitment to the Indian and Pakistani administrative services, has now disappeared in Malaya. Since the availability of qualified degree holders has not yet exceeded the demand—a point that was reached in India prior to World War II—and since suitable administrative talent in the subordinate bureaucracy is scarce, recruitment has proceeded almost automatically in Malaya with formal qualifications and the approval of the Public Services Commission being the major criteria for selection. Today, faith in the examination process is evidenced only in the routine confirmation examination that must be successfully completed before the probationary MCS officer is placed on the permanent establishment, but the nature of this examination is itself revealing of the nature of one aspect of the administrative services and therefore deserves at least brief consideration.

While the competitive qualification examination of the ICS type is intended to eliminate from consideration those not acceptable in the eyes of the bureaucratic system, the confirmation examination is designed to assure that those already accepted will learn (and presumably apply) the same rules of conduct and behavior practiced by other members of the system. In addition to one or more language papers, the major emphasis in the MCS confirmation examination is on laws and regulations. There is a total of five three-hour papers dealing with penal laws, criminal procedure, general laws, *General Orders, Financial General Orders,* and the *Manual of Office Procedure.*[7] There is great emphasis on laws and rules of procedure, and in fact the nature of the

6. See chap. ii, n. 25.
7. See Federation of Malaya, Federation Establishment Office, *Circular Letter* 5694/29, "Revision of Syllabus for MCS Law Examination" (Kuala Lumpur: typescript, 1958).

questions actually given in the confirmation examinations of 1957–60 (the only ones to which the author has had access) seems to suggest that the ideal MCS officer is envisaged as a vast storage bin of regulations from which, given the proper stimulus, he can immediately extract the appropriate rule. The examination process then serves the twofold purpose of encouraging individual officers to approximate the ideal as closely as possible, at the same time serving as an obstacle in the path of potential non-conformists. So much faith is placed in the efficacy of the confirmation examination that an MCS recruit, regardless of his academic qualifications or experience, cannot begin the orderly rise up the ladder of seniority until he has first cleared this hurdle.

Thus the MCS has basically conformed to the ICS model in the sense that it is a service of administrative generalists, who in large measure owe their positions not only to formal academic qualifications but also to their successes on written examinations. Moreover, both services are elitist—that is, the officers of both regard themselves as being the most senior of the senior bureaucracy, a ranking that is also generally accepted by their technical and professional colleagues as well as by the general public whom they serve. This elitism claimed and recognized in the MCS is not unqualified, but a further discussion of this topic requires a closer examination of the general nature and ethos of the MCS.

III. The Character of the Contemporary MCS

The superiority of the MCS has been recognized within as well as outside the bureaucracy, but the extremes of this elitist demeanor observed in the Civil Service of Pakistan is not evident in Malaya.[8] Perhaps much of this spirit existed in the years prior to World War II, but the MCS that re-emerged after the Japanese

8. The CSP is the lineal descendent of the ICS in Pakistan. This generalization is based on the author's observations during a brief visit to the Civil Service Academy in Lahore and on conversations with Professor R. J. Braibanti of Duke University, who previously served as Chief Adviser to the Academy. There seems to be a vast attitudinal difference between the average officer of the MCS and that of the CSP.

occupation was not the same service that staffed the administrative posts in 1941. It would be a gross exaggeration to suggest that an egalitarian spirit pervades the MCS of today, for it does not, but it would also be inaccurate to think of the contemporary MCS in the same terms as the CSP and the Indian Administrative Service. The MCS enjoys great prestige, and its members constitute some of the genuine administrative elite of Malaya, but these members are generally able to accept the prestige gracefully without invoking the symbolic trappings of superiority that were characteristic of the prewar Service.[9]

Undoubtedly many factors combined to make the MCS less elite conscious than it was in an earlier period, and among these the Japanese occupation of Malaya (and the resulting disruption of colonial administration) is probably one of the most important. It can be shown statistically that the occupation drastically altered the composition of the MCS. Moreover, though this is considerably more difficult to document, it seems probable that the internment of senior and junior officers together during the occupation—or the necessity of being subject to common restrictions where internment did not occur—brought about a general social leveling among the returning personnel that did not take place in the Indian Subcontinent. In addition, the interregnum of the British Military Administration (1945–46), a period of shortages and hardships, made a positive virtue of one's willingness to roll up his sleeves and get to work, and the BMA itself was staffed largely by administrative officers with little or no previous MCS experience, who were later to enter the Service by way of the "administrative officers pool." While such changes in personal attitudes cannot be quantified after the event is over, statistics alone can account to a great extent for many of the attitudinal changes in the MCS.

Of 238 MCS officers in 1947, 107 (44.9 per cent) had seen no previous service in Malaya. Of the 49 officers who held senior posts in 1941, only 14 appeared on the *Staff List* of 1947, the first

9. It seems significant that the only serious attempts to revive some of the prewar symbolism have come not from expatriate officers but from Malayans of the older group who reached political maturity in the MAS under the watchful eyes of their expatriate MCS superiors in the years preceding the Japanese occupation.

postwar year for which such information is available. Since many of the new administrative officers had records of military service, the average age of MCS officers did not vary greatly between the prewar and the postwar Service,[10] but the average length of service in Malaya shows a marked decline when the two periods are compared. In 1940 senior MCS officers had served in Malaya an average of 26.4 years, while in 1947 this figure had dropped to 21.5 (much of which did not include MCS service). The most significant comparison, however, may be made in the junior posts, where the day-to-day contacts with Malay subordinates and general public took place. In this group, men who were shortly to become the senior administrative officers of the Peninsula, the average length of service in Malaya had dropped from the 1940 figure of 12.6 years to the 1947 level of 5.4 years. It is perhaps even more revealing that among these subordinate expatriate officers of the MCS, 55 per cent had not seen any previous service in Malaya.

From these statistics it is possible to conclude that the Japanese occupation caused the introduction into Malaya of a somewhat younger officer, certainly one who felt less of the historic colonial attachment for Malaya, and perhaps one therefore who was less attracted to the colonial symbols and customs. Just as the MCS uniform and the formal dinner dress disappeared with the occupation, so too did many of the attitudes that these costumes symbolized.

The communal nature of the MCS is an aspect of the senior service that may be treated only briefly, for it is statistically apparent and well recognized in Malaya that the Service is primarily Malay and not Malayan. As Table 20 demonstrated, Malays account for more than three-fourths the total membership of the

10. Data in this paragraph have been tabulated by the author from Straits Settlements and FMS, *The Malayan Civil List, 1940* (Singapore: Government Printing Office, 1940); Straits Settlements and FMS, *Malayan Establishment Staff List as on 1st July, 1941* (Singapore: Government Printing Office, 1941); and Malayan Union, *Malayan Establishment Staff List, 31st December 1947* (Kuala Lumpur: Government Press, 1948). The particular copy of the 1941 *Staff List* employed here had been altered in ink to reflect personnel changes on the eve of the Japanese invasion. Figures given above include these changes. Among the senior MCS officers, the average ages in 1940 and 1947 were 50.7 and 50.5 years respectively; among the junior, 38.0 and 34.7.

MCS, and a recruitment ratio of four Malays to each non-Malay assures that this approximate relationship will be maintained in future years.[11] The results of this Malay "handicap" [12] are readily apparent; its implications are less obvious. There is no doubt that this better-than-even break provides opportunities for recruitment into the senior administrative service for many Malays who probably could not otherwise have expected to become MCS officers; as a result it is likely the success of these Malays, together with the other methods of encouragement employed by the government, may in turn be bringing more Malays out of their traditional way of life and into modern Malaya. Yet it also seems probable that these quotas may have some less beneficial side effects. One major disadvantage is that there is a serious shortage of "high level manpower," to borrow a phrase of Frederick Harbison from a report on Nigerian education,[13] and any scheme that fails to maximize the utilization of these scarce human resources is itself irrational in terms of the nation's long-range economic goals. The second undesirable side effect concerns individual attitudes and is thus more conjecture than pure observation, but personal conversations suggest that there is the danger that Malays might come to regard these quotas as part of their birthright, and this temporary stimulant might then become a permanent opiate. Moreover, in the long run, Malays may find that recruitment quotas into the MCS can also provide unexpected handicaps for the non-Malay communities. Even if all other conditions were equal, it is statistically probable that a non-Malay would have to be four times more qualified than a Malay if he were to be acceptable in the eyes of the MCS. Thus, if the objectivity of the organs of internal administration of the bureauc-

11. The original quota was imposed at the time that the MCS was first opened to non-Malays in 1953. (See the original proposal as put forward by the then High Commissioner [General Sir Gerald Templer] in Federation of Malaya, Federal Legislative Council [Fifth Session], *Proceedings* [Kuala Lumpur: Government Press, 1953], pp. 473–74.) Quotas employed today have been sanctioned by the Constitution. (See chap. iv, above, n. 31.)

12. Minister of Finance Tan Siew Sin is reported to have said that "special privileges are like a golf handicap. They are not to hold the Chinese down but to help the Malays along." See *Time*, April 12, 1963, p. 43.

13. See his "Human Resources and Economic Development in Nigeria," in Robert O. Tilman and Taylor Cole, eds., *The Nigerian Political Scene* (Durham, N.C.: Duke University Press, 1962), pp. 198–219.

racy continues, it seems not unlikely that positions of major responsibility may increasingly be assigned to those most qualified for the posts, and in time it may be discovered that while the MCS is still predominantly Malay in character, the decision-making process could be monopolized by a group that is disproportionately non-Malay.

Another characteristic of the MCS that should be noted is that it suffers today from the effects of a split personality. The two extremes are represented by the older officers of the Malay College-MAS tradition, on the one hand, and by the younger officers recruited directly from the universities, on the other. The basic values of the two groups are probably similar, in the sense that they both have been socialized into the same political game and are willing to abide by approximately the same rules of the game. But the two differing socialization processes have left their marks on individual personalities of the older and younger officers, and these individuals together help to shape the character of the MCS just as they in turn are influenced by the Service. At the present time the dominant ethos of the MCS is determined by representatives of the older tradition, for of the 53 superscale officers on the establishment in 1962, 79 per cent had entered the MCS by promotion from the MAS, 11 per cent had come through a state civil service, 8 per cent were from other subordinate services, and only 2 per cent (a single officer) had been recruited directly from a university without first passing through a junior segment of the bureaucracy.[14] Thus, more than three fourths of the total superscale officers of the MCS have served an apprenticeship in the junior administrative service, and it was through this instrument that many of the fundamental values of the colonial officer of the ICS type were transmitted.

Created in 1910 to provide indigenous officers to staff the subordinate administrative posts, the MAS originally drew probationers only from Malay College at Kuala Kangsar, an English-language secondary school established by the colonial administration that

14. See the author's "Policy Formulation, Policy Execution, and the Political Elite Structure of Contemporary Malaya," in Wang Gunwu, ed., *Malaysia* (London: Pall Mall Ltd., in press), Table 55.

attempted to duplicate the curriculum and environment of an English public school.[15] The MAS itself never enjoyed a position of real importance in the bureaucratic structure, for it has always been what it was in 1910—a junior administrative service. However, in its role as a reservoir of native talent on which the MCS could draw, the MAS has been disproportionately influential in shaping the character of the present-day MCS. In fact the older MCS officers of today are the last representatives of the ethos of the prewar expatriate administrators, and they have assumed this role largely as a result of their experiences in the MAS.[16]

A lengthy quotation from a speech by a senior MCS officer before a group of newly recruited administrative personnel in 1959 demonstrates the character and outlook of the older MCS officers of the Malay College–MAS tradition:

> I should like to talk to you this morning on the responsibilities which you must now shoulder outside office hours. Many of you are members of the Malayan Civil Service, the most senior service in this country. Others of you are members of the Malay Administrative Service and the State Civil Services but I trust that you also aspire, in your hearts, to eventual promotion to the Malayan Civil Service. The Malayan Civil Service is a service with great traditions which has produced many important figures in this country. . . .
> It will be impossible for you in your life outside the office to be

15. Though established originally to train the "sons of Malays of the Raja and higher classes," Malay College was eventually opened to somewhat broader enrollment and became the leading secondary school in Malaya. (On the creation of the College, and the source from which the above quotation is derived, see Straits Settlements, *Report for 1910 on the Federated Malay States*, p. 23, in Great Britain, *Accounts and Papers, 1911*, Vol. 53, Cd. 5902.) Even today, six of the eleven Rulers and Governors of the constituent states of the Federation were educated at Malay College, while a majority of the 53 superscale officers of the MCS have also come from this background. A study of the socializing influence of Malay College could probably enhance considerably our understanding of British-Malay relations.

16. During the stay of probationers at Malay College and throughout their careers in the MAS and MCS, the conduct of Malay officers both on and off the job would be carefully watched. Older Malay officers of the present MCS have sometimes commented with a note of seriousness that "proper" manner and habits were greater assets than administrative competence. It has been reported that the social graces of Malay subordinates were the subject of careful and methodic study, and a major promotion recommendation would include an appraisal of this aspect of the officer's potential. In some cases older officers might have romanticized about the importance of "correct" manners, but there seems to be little doubt that some weight was placed on the question of social fitness and that this qualification was measured on an almost completely English scale.

regarded, by your friends and by the general public, in any other way than as an officer of the Malayan Civil Service. This status makes it essential that you should always behave in a manner befitting a senior Government officer. You may not as yet be very senior in length of service but you must never forget that you have a certain standard to maintain. All of us have to have some form of relaxation. While a particular celebration may include an infrequent visit to a cabaret it is certainly not proper for an MCS officer to make cabarets his usual form of amusement. In the social circle you will have to choose your friends carefully so that no one can say that you are in a position to show favour to them in your official capacity. While there is every reason that you should be civil and on good terms with members of the general public it is certainly not desirable that you should always be seen in the company of *towkays* and the business officials.

You must strive to maintain your dignity, to be honest and above all try to avoid a situation in which you are open even to the faintest breath of suspicion about your integrity. . . . I can assure you that your behavior outside office hours will be almost as important a factor to your senior officers in recommending your promotion in the service as will be your performance in office during office hours.

I would like you to realize that the Service to which you should be proud to belong has a very high tradition, and indeed is the best Service in any of the East Asian countries. This reputation has been built up over a period of nearly three quarters of a century by men who dedicated themselves to the principles I have already described to you. They went through untold hardships, restraints and selfless devotion in order to defend and uphold those principles. As their successors you must not let them down.[17]

While these older officers still set the tone of the MCS, younger officers are coming less and less from the subordinate services and are increasingly recruited directly from the universities, a trend that is already well established and one that will probably become more marked as the number of available graduates grows in the coming years. As of January 1, 1962, of the 204 Malayan time-scale officers, 44 per cent had been recruited through the MAS, while an almost identical 43 per cent had entered the Service directly from the universities.[18] Moreover, even those who came

17. Note some of the similarities here to the comments made in n. 16, above.
18. The remaining officers have entered the MCS by promotion from the state civil services. See the essay cited in note 14, above. At the time these tabulations were made, only seven Malayan members holding degrees from foreign universities had been recruited directly into the MCS. The remainder of the officers

from the MAS probably could not be said to represent the Malay College–MAS tradition illustrated above. The demands of Malayanization decimated the ranks of the MAS in the early stages of the program, and most of the officers promoted into the MCS from the MAS in later years had entered the junior administrative service through another Division II or III service and represented individuals who under more normal circumstances probably would never have reached the senior service.

To recognize a different spirit among the younger group of university graduates is relatively simple, but to define and analyze these differences is considerably more difficult. In general, the officers of the older MAS tradition seem more intent on retaining the ways of the expatriate, are less willing to innovate or even to listen to suggestions for innovations, and are quick to invoke the custom of colonial practice to legitimatize their conservatism. In a sense, of course, this only reflects human nature, and similar examples can probably be found in almost any established bureaucracy in the world. It is only that the differences become more marked in a country where the older generation has been socialized into the colonial administrative environment and has been so closely connected with their expatriate tutors while the younger generation of university graduates have undergone only an indirect colonial experience. The older bureaucrats had become so accustomed to colonial paternalism that when the colonials departed they often turned somewhat blindly for guidance to the written legacy left behind by their former superiors—the rules and regulations that still constitute the guidelines for the conduct of bureaucracy. This subject, however, more appropriately belongs to a discussion of role of the MCS in the total political system, for as the bureaucratic elite the MCS was often as political as it was administrative.

entering directly with university degrees had come from the University of Singapore (formerly the University of Malaya at Singapore). The new University of Malaya (Kuala Lumpur) had not (as of January 1, 1962) provided any recruits for the MCS. Of the superscale MCS officers discussed above, only five held degrees from foreign universities or had completed studies at the Inns of Court in London. (These tabulations have been derived from records of the University of Singapore, interviews, and inquiries.)

IV. Conclusion: The Administrative Services and the Political Process

The role of the administrative services in the political process is one of contrasts, for both the MCS and the MAS represent a conservative as well as an innovative force. They are conservative in the sense that they have provided one of the most important channels of political socialization and in no small measure have been responsible for the perpetuation of the modern political culture after the departure of the Europeans. In more narrow terms both services exhibit considerable conservatism in adhering to colonial practices that may no longer seem applicable and in any case may never have been so sacrosanct as they are now regarded. Yet, at the other extreme, the MCS does furnish some of the political elite [19] of Malaya, albeit an elite that is sometimes reluctant to exert its full potential for influence.

(1) *The Socialization Function of the Administrative Services*

Discussion in preceding paragraphs has been adequate to demonstrate the socializing influence of the MAS on the present MCS, and it remains only to examine the contribution of the administrative services to the socialization of the other elite groups.[20] Note the importance of the bureaucracy as a channel of elite recruitment within one group.

19. "Political elite" is used throughout this section as a generic category under which might be subsumed more specific classifications of elites, such as "bureaucratic, elected and party, royal, military, and commercial." The generic term is defined as "individuals or groups clustered within or around the structures of government who are able to exert influence disproportionate to their numbers in the formulation and execution of government policy." See the author's "Policy Formulation, Policy Execution, and the Political Elite Structure of Contemporary Malaya," for a discussion of modern elite theories. On the limitations on actions of elites, see especially note 2.

20. While the nature of the socialization process has been discussed, it might also be suggestive to point out the magnitude of this function. Of 53 superscale MCS officers on the establishment in 1962, 45 per cent had 16–25 years of service, and 40 per cent had 26–35 years. For a table giving the complete statistics, see *ibid.*, Table 3.

Table 31. *Elected and Party Elite: Avenues of Recruitment* *

Avenue	Cabinet-Party $n = 13$	Cabinet $n = 18$	Party $n = 33$	Total Elite $n = 38$
Bureaucracy	46	50	39	42
Professions	23	22	15	16
Business	23	22	24	24
Other	0	0	12	11
Unknown	8	6	9	8

* Figures given are percentages. For source and explanation of categories, see "Policy Formulation, Policy Execution, and the Political Elite Structure of Contemporary Malaya," *passim*, esp. Table 53.

To this it may also be added that five of the present eleven rulers and governors of the states of the Federation have had some experience in the administrative bureaucracy. To a great extent modernity came to Malaya and is perpetuated by the vehicle of the bureaucracy, and within the total bureaucracy the MAS and MCS have assumed primary importance in the function of socialization.

(2) *The Administrative Services as Adherents of Colonial Rules*

Lucian Pye has perceptively pointed out that much of Southeast Asia enjoys the belief that good government depends upon the mechanical application of rules and that the rule books still in use are largely those created by the colonial powers. Yet, Pye further argues, this is based on a mistaken understanding of the place of regulations during the colonial administration.

In actual practice, the system did not work in an entirely mechanistic fashion. The colonial officials generally made what they considered the appropriate decision in conformity with the spirit of the regulations as they understood them. The skill of the clerks, more often than not, was finding suitable regulations to support the decisions of their superiors. In a sense, these colonial officials stood slightly aloof from the machinery of administration, so that they could reach in and tinker with the machine in order to ensure that it operated in an efficient and effective manner.[21]

Perhaps in future years, as the younger officers replace those with a more personal colonial experience, the bureaucratic elites of the MCS will demonstrate somewhat greater flexibility, but for the present time it is too often that the absence of an appropriate regulation, or the conflict of two rules—after considerable delay—only produces a new regulation. The machine grinds on, and only relatively few of the senior bureaucrats are willing to reach in and tinker with its seemingly intricate inner workings.

(3) *The MCS as a Political Elite: The District Officer*

The DO in Malaya probably never enjoyed the policy-making discretion of his ICS colleague in the Indian Subcontinent since the country was more compact, the districts were smaller and closer to the administrative capital, and—most important—simply because he arrived on the colonial scene at a much later date in history, after better means of communication had been developed to keep him in touch with his superiors in Kuala Lumpur and they in turn with Singapore.[22] Yet, it is more a difference of degree than of kind, for in the Malayan colonial DO were also combined many legislative, executive and judicial powers, which in turn made the DO almost as political as he was administrative, and it was this tradition that was passed on to the MCS District Officer after independence.

The modern DO is caught simultaneously in several dilemmas. He is often viewed from Kuala Lumpur as a post office for receiving government policies and for transmitting upward information and intelligence about his district. By the accepted

21. Lucian W. Pye, "Southeast Asia," in Gabriel A. Almond and James S. Coleman, *The Politics of the Developing Areas* (Princeton: Princeton University Press, 1960), pp. 144–45.
22. It should be remembered that by 1909, only thirteen years after the implementation of the Federated Malay States, it was possible to travel by rail between the mainland opposite Penang and Singapore in less than a day and to send messages by telegraph over the same route in a matter of several minutes. See chap. ii, tables 11 and 13, above.

canons of administration he rules his district as a Platonic guardian, but he is now surrounded by a federal structure, a democratic constitution, and an elected Federal Government that puts considerable emphasis on the development of viable local government and popularly elected local bodies. He is an official appointed by the Federal Government; except for an informal veto of a posting, local councils have no control over the selection of a DO. As a result, the relationships between the DO and the locally elected officials are likely to be dependent more upon the relative dominance of personalities than upon any institutional factors. Basically, the two ideas of government seem contradictory, and it is left to the individuals to work out a *modus vivendi* in each case. Where a locally elected leader or council dominates, the DO is likely to slip into the background and serve chiefly as a means of informing Kuala Lumpur of activities in the district, but where the DO is predominant the structure of government permits a form of direction not unlike the period of colonial administration.

Except during the height of the Emergency, when DO's were called upon for many duties not normally connected with district administration, the work of the post-independence District Officer has been concerned largely with problems of land administration. As the introductory chapter pointed out, land administration is still in an unhealthy state in Malaya, and the interruption of the Emergency can be blamed only in part for this condition. While the appropriateness of the DO system of land administration might be questioned,[23] it is nevertheless evident that this aspect of the work of the DO is most responsible for placing the citizenry of the outlying areas in direct contact with an officer of the Federal Government. Land administration itself is of course contained on the state list of the Constitution, but the guiding direction of the Federation's land policies comes from Kuala Lumpur,[24] and these are executed chiefly by officers who have a strong Federal Government orientation.

23. It was seriously questioned by the Land Administration Commission in 1958. See chap. i, n. 49, above.
24. On the constitutional position of land administration, see chap. i, n. 50, above.

(4) *The MCS as a Political Elite: The Federal Officer*

Members of the MCS are part of Malaya's political elite in the sense that government policy decisions are often greatly influenced by the views and desires of MCS officers. Permanent Secretaries and Secretaries to ministries have an intimate knowledge of the over-all workings of the structure of government, and Principal Assistant Secretaries and Assistant Secretaries often have the technical and administrative expertise necessary to make policy suggestions that may eventually become policy decisions. While recognizing that MCS officers are members of the generic category "political elite," it would nevertheless be hazardous to defend any thesis that their power position is superior (or inferior) to that of any or all of the other elite groups. In Malaya it is apparently impossible at the present time to visualize the political process as a contest for power among contending elite groups, for in fact all of the dominant groups have passed through approximately the same process of political socialization, all speak the same political language (in form as well as in meaning),[25] all are playing approximately the same political game for about the same reasons, and all are abiding by roughly the same rules of the political game. Moreover, there is a particularly close kinship between the bureaucratic elite and the elected and party elites, for a significant number of the latter have had considerable bureaucratic experience, and this usually represents experience gained in one or both of the administrative services.[26] Bureaucratic and elected elites have been recruited from similar sources,[27] and in both of

25. For statistical support of this generalization, see "Policy Formulation, Policy Execution, and the Political Elite Structure of Contemporary Malaya," Tables 50 and 51.
26. See Table 31, above.
27. Among the total elected and party elite (n = 38), 47 per cent have had some university, college, or Inns of Court experience, while 37 per cent have not gone beyond a secondary education (unknown = 17 per cent). Of the total Malayan officers of the MCS (n = 257), 43 per cent have been recruited directly from the universities, while 58 per cent have been promoted from the subordinate services. This latter group contains a very small (but unfortunately unknown) number of degree holders. For the breakdown of these figures by junior and senior elite groups, see pp. 111, 113, above.

these groups the more Malayan-oriented Malays seem to be pre-dominant.[28]

It is only within the context of this consensus among the elite groups that it is possible to speak of the bureaucratic neutrality of the MCS in the Weberian sense. In the present elite structure the MCS is indeed neutral, but it does not necessarily follow that this represents absolute neutrality. It may, or it may not. The simple fact is that its neutrality has never been tested, and unless the character of one or more of the other elite groups is altered in the course of time in a manner not similarly reflected in the MCS elite, the neutrality of the senior administrative service is not likely to be tested.

28. The primarily Malay composition is easy to document; the attitude of the elite toward communal questions is not. On the MCS, see chap. iii, Table 20, above. Of the 38 individuals classified as elected and party elite, 24 are Malay. (See "Policy Formulation, Policy Execution, and the Political Elite Structure of Contemporary Malaya.") The nine Malay Rulers of the Federation are of course Malay by tradition and definition; in addition, the appointed Governors of Penang and Malacca at the present time are also Malay, though this is not a formal requirement and previous Governors have on occasion been Chinese. The "Malayan orientation" suggested above is meant to imply that most of the elites tend to play down the importance of communal affiliations and to play up the pan-communal nature of Malayan government. This characteristic of Malayan elites cannot be documented at the present time.

6

Malayan Bureaucracy: The Process of Change and the Future

Malayan bureaucracy was a manifestation of social and political change as well as an agency of change. The progressive development of the bureaucratic machine was occasioned by social and economic demands, but at the same time bureaucrats and bureaucratic practices stimulated new demands and increased existing ones. While it is apparent that the two processes went hand-in-hand, it will be our purpose here to analyze the manner in which the bureaucracy and the bureaucratic structures changed over time, keeping in mind however that at the same time it served as a stimulus, a catalyst, and a barometer.

I. Bureaucracy in Transition: The Broad Perspective

This section, following some suggested research leads by Joseph LaPalombara,[1] will employ three dimensions of political change

1. "Bureaucracy and Political Development: Notes, Queries, and Dilemmas," in LaPalombara, ed., *Bureaucracy and Political Development*, chap. ii. It should be made clear that these dimensions are probably not employed here in precisely the same manner for which they were intended by Professor LaPalombara. One of the two major questions raised by Professor LaPalombara is "whether it makes any sense—whether it is useful—to think about development or change in terms of some conception of the politically 'modern,' whatever may be the attributes that one ascribes to 'modernity.'" His answer to this question is in the negative and he therefore submits as a substitute four dimensions for analysis. Professor LaPalombara's major criticisms of the "modernity" model are as follows: (1) its meaning lacks concreteness and it is used to mean many things to many people, both among the various disciplines as well as within each discipline; (2) the "concept is often implicitly and perhaps unintentionally normative" since it suggests "that those political systems are 'modern' which possess the structural and behavioral

as an orienting framework for presenting a general overview of Malayan bureaucratic development.[2]

(1) *Degree of Structural Differentiation*

The general development of the political system from pre-European to contemporary Malaya has been characterized by the progressive differentiation of functions, which in turn has been accompanied by the creation and refinement of increasingly differentiated structures for carrying out these functions. In the Malaya of the Hindu rulers and the Malay Sultans there was little attempt to differentiate between politics, administration, religion, and economics. The ruler usually saw himself as a political decision-maker and as head of the religious community. His social subordinates (though sometimes his political equals) were in one sense his administrative staff, but at the same time they—particularly the territorial chiefs—were as involved in politics and economics as was the ruler, and often even more involved. Even when limiting our observations to the administrative functions of District Chiefs, it is apparent that they were all things to all men. A chief might be called upon to be the arbiter of disputes among his lieutenants or he might be the final appeal for judging the validity of sanctions imposed at a lower level. As the collector of taxes in his district he had financial responsibilities, and in determining the portion of these to remit to the ruler he was able to extend his influence beyond the territorial limits of his own area.

---

attributes that can be associated with the Anglo-American democracy"; and (3) the use of "modernity" suggests "a single, final state of affairs—a deterministic, unilinear theory of political evolution" (pp. 35–39). As I have suggested in chap. i, we are indeed limited in our perceptive powers by our own experiences and thus we tend to equate "modernity" to an ideal abstraction of our present society. However, as I have earlier suggested, there seem to be some convincing arguments for positing an ideal abstraction of our present society as a hypothetical model, if it is always kept in mind that models are not reality; they are useful as tools of analysis but they should invite destruction just as much as progressive refinement. Moreover, Professor LaPalombara has posited four dimensions, each of which implicitly has two opposite abstractions placed at the ends of a continuum, and taken together it might be argued that they constitute some of the major characteristics of the tradition-modernity dichotomy suggested in chap. i. It is for this reason that I have adopted his dimensions without accepting his rejection of the larger model.

2. The dimension "magnitude" is also applicable, but reliable statistics on the size and intensity of Malayan bureaucracy are not available prior to 1956.

The structures of government, including those of administration, were as undifferentiated in traditional Malaya as were the functions they fulfilled. Whether it might have been the *penghulu* and the council of elders at the village level, the district chief and his trusted advisers, or the ruler with his four ranks of ministers, each level of government incorporated within itself all the functions of government in largely undifferentiated institutions.

When the English East India Company first began to trade, and later to hold jurisdiction over territory to facilitate trade, its structures and functions were almost as undifferentiated as those of traditional Malaya. Initially a ship's captain was commander of the vessel, paymaster, judge, chief merchant, and occasionally physician and surgeon. The line of authority extended downward from the captain, and—though there was an increasing tendency for officers exclusively to fill jobs for which they were best suited or needed—in each subordinate was combined the same assortment of powers vested ultimately in the captain. As the business of the Company became more complex the structure of the organization became increasingly differentiated. In London this manifested itself in the creation of the General Court, Court of Directors, Board of Control, and the Secret Committee. In the field the merchant-captain gave way to the residential merchants and the seafaring captains, and the functions of the former were further divided and subdivided. By the time of the arrival of the British in Malayan waters there were covenanted and uncovenanted servants, and these were further classified according to functional role—senior merchants, junior merchants, factors, warehousemen, writers, etc. At the policy-making level in the field, councils were eventually established; these were later to serve as models for the colonial legislative councils, under the direction of the senior-most Company servant, the Governor in the case of the Presidency and the Resident Councillor in the case of subordinate units. These councils at first were composed exclusively of company servants, who were also the senior merchants, and thus together in the policy-making body were representatives of the administrative and economic structures of government.

It was during the period of colonial administration in Malaya

(1867–1957) that the process of functional and structural differentiation accelerated most rapidly. Demands caused an increase in services performed, and these increased activities generated greater demands. The policy-making structure (later to be called the Legislative Council) became increasingly separated from the institutions of administration as there was a progressive diminution of *ex officio* membership and an increasing emphasis on, first, appointed, and later, elected membership. The major structural break between the economic and the political-administrative functions of government in Malaya might be regarded as occurring in 1858 when the English East India Company ceased to exist formally and its duties were assumed by the Crown directly, though, of course, the Company had long before become more concerned with civil and military administration than with trade. This trend continued throughout the colonial period as bureaucrats became increasingly reluctant to be identified with the commercial classes, whether they might have been Asian immigrants or fellow countrymen. The last stronghold of structural and functional fusion in the bureaucracy was the District Officer, in whom one might find combined the powers of the magistrate, revenue collector, land settlement officer, political leader, and often personal confidant, mentor, adviser, and medical attendant. Much of this undifferentiated structure remained throughout the colonial and into the independent period, but the actual discretionary power of the DO decreased with the growth of modern medical, educational, and judicial services, and with the creation of the posts of Commissioners of Lands and Mines together with the delegation of actual land administration responsibilities to the Assistant District Officer.

The process of structural-functional differentiation has continued throughout the independent period, and even the major repository of the idea of undifferentiated administrative generalists—the Malayan Civil Service—has not been left untouched. Magistral duties have increasingly devolved upon the Judicial and Legal Service, which was itself an institutional outgrowth of the MCS. By 1959 it had been officially recognized that many officers in the MCS would be forced to begin specialization early in their careers and that technical competency in a given field would necessarily be a factor in promotion recommendations.[3] This only confirmed by regulation what had become accepted in practice, for in the independent MCS it was becoming increasingly unusual for officers to be passed through the field into ministerial posts and thereafter from one functional post to another of a totally unrelated nature.

(2) Degree of Achievement Orientation

From Confucian bureaucratic practice to Max Weber's ideal type, it has usually been argued that bureaucratic recruitment and role assignment *ought* to be achievemental and not ascriptive in orientation. The actual and the ideal [4] have often failed to coincide in Malaya as well as in the rest of the world, though it seems significant that from the time of the East India Company onward there has seldom failed to be some recognition that ascriptive criteria constituted the least desirable basis for recruitment, assignment, and promotion.

In traditional Hindu and Muslim Malaya there is little evidence of concern about the criteria of selection for political and administrative service. A ruler was the ruler because he had inherited the privilege, he was the eldest, or because he was by nature the most influential. Ultimate authority was based on religion, magic, and ritual, and those in positions to manipulate these forces to serve their own ends were vested with great political power. Succession of posts was usually determined ascriptively by birth, though it is apparent that the outcome of contests for power often altered the lines of succession. Role assignments, in addition to being controlled by privileges of birth, were also influenced by the necessity of conforming to certain cosmological principles,

---

3. Federation of Malaya, *General Circular No. 4 of 1959,* "Organization within Ministries" (Kuala Lumpur: Government Press, 1959), par. 20.
4. Here I am using "ideal" in the sense of an abstraction, not in the normative sense of being the "best." Recent scholarship has in fact questioned the previously accepted norm of achievemental recruitment as being the "best" for all societies. See Fred W. Riggs, "Bureaucrats and Political Development: A Paradoxical View," in LaPalombara, ed., *Bureaucracy and Political Development,* chap. v.

and in the promotion of *mentris* and territorial officials magic and ritual continued to play a dominant role. Thus, those vested with religious and magic authority were ordained to rule; those without these qualities were destined to be ruled.

Selection of Company servants was at first based entirely on patronage, with the result that personal and family contacts governed appointment rather than any universal criteria. While this was the accepted practice, it nevertheless was true that the Court of Directors—and later Parliament—became increasingly concerned about the obvious abuses of the privileges of recruitment, assignment, and promotion. As a result, the first rules governing procedures for recruitment into the senior posts were inserted into the Charter Act of 1793, and from that point until the present time the trend in Malayan bureaucracy has been to diminish the extent to which ascriptive factors influence recruitment. Beginning with crude affidavits denying under oath and bond any nepotism or nefarious connections, the bureaucracy has seen the continual creation of procedures and techniques intended to minimize the influence of birth and associations in recruitment and to maximize the criterion of ability as the basis for entering the administrative services.

Tracing the movement from particular to universal recruitment norms becomes more complex during the Colonial Office period of Malayan history, particularly after the time that local officers began to staff some of the senior posts. Though from 1869 to 1882 examinations were open only to those selected to sit for them by the Secretary of State for the Colonies, great emphasis was placed on the examination method of recruitment until the examination system—originally established for the Indian Civil Service —was abandoned in 1930 by the Eastern Cadet Service (which included Malaya). Even after the abolition of the open examination universal criteria continued to be the sought-after goals in the recruitment of European servants, and certain practices provided a rational means of at least partially attaining this goal.

It is at the level of local recruitment, however, that an examination of the degree of achievemental orientation of the bureaucracy becomes infinitely more complex. Except for the occasional

Malay studying abroad who sat for the general examination in London, recruitment of native officers to the senior bureaucracy was almost entirely at the discretion of local colonial officials. In the Malayan Civil Service it was more institutionalized, since Malays, for many years, could enter the MCS only by promotion from the Malay Administrative Service, and in turn could qualify for the MAS only after successful completion of Malay College at Kuala Kangsar. In this sense then, for Malays, there was an element of achievement involved, for one could not expect consideration for an MCS post unless he first had the Malay College–MAS experience.[5] Yet the standard of recruitment was still based primarily on ascriptive factors despite the slight bow in the direction of personal achievement. This is true for at least three reasons. First, only Malays were recruited for the most senior posts (MCS) until 1953; thus a non-Malay resident of Malaya could not become an MCS officer regardless of his ability. Second, according to official policy, Malay College was created for the Raja and higher classes, and though in more recent years it has been opened to Malay commoners on a quota basis, it nevertheless meant that almost throughout the period of indirect recruitment into the MCS only the children of Malay royalty could have the opportunity to prove their ability. Third, even for those who met the ascriptive qualifications for entrance into Malay College and the MAS, selection for the MCS was not based entirely on achievemental factors. Social fitness was almost as important as administrative ability in the process of selection, and the pre-war MAS officer who did not appreciate English tea and could not intelligently discuss the fine points of cricket was not a likely candidate for the MCS.

The bureaucracy of independent Malaya continues to put forward as a desideratum the goal of recruitment, role assignment, and promotion based on achievemental norms, but it has also inherited part of the ascriptive standards left behind by the departing colonials. Although recruitment examinations are not in

5. Recruitment into the MAS was broadened to take in other institutions in 1921, but the majority of all MAS probationers continued to come from Malay College until after World War II.

general use in Malaya, the Public Services Commission does make a considerable effort to enforce universal standards of recruitment and to guarantee that applicants do in fact possess the minimum qualifications prescribed for the various services. Since there have usually been more available posts than there are qualified applicants, there is considerably less reason for qualifying examinations than one might find in India and Pakistan, for example. While ascriptive selection has undoubtedly been practiced on some occasions even at this higher level of recruitment, objectivity and neutrality have remained the goal with certain general but important limitations.

Just as the colonial bureaucracy found it desirable to utilize general ascriptive criteria in the process of prerecruitment selection, so has the independent government considered it necessary that this should be continued. Recruitment quotas exist today just as they did in 1953, and these are designed to encourage Malays and discourage non-Malays. Yet, even acknowledging this apparent withdrawal from an achievement orientation, it is still possible to argue that the general trend has been away from ascriptive recruitment and toward achievemental recruitment. Prior to World War II an indigenous officer in a senior policy-making position was the rare exception, for these posts were almost the complete preserve of the British. Moreover, while there were many Malay officers in the administrative services, the number of non-Malay officers holding posts even of similar salary (not to mention prestige and influence) was small indeed. Since independence, though recruitment quotas are still imposed in certain small but key services, statistics presented in preceding chapters demonstrate that communal origins no longer play the important ascriptive role that they did in earlier years. Thus, so far as one important ascriptive criterion is concerned, the trend from traditional to modern times has clearly been in the direction of an increased acceptance of achievemental recruitment and—to a less extent—role assignment.

When we move from a discussion of communal ties to other more modern political affiliations we are less able to be certain about trends toward or away from achievemental recruitment to the bureaucracy. All senior Malayan bureaucrats, regardless of communal origins, are followers of the Alliance Party in the same sense that all American bureaucrats are democrats with a small "d." There is a general political consensus underlying the Alliance, and, though it is always in danger of losing support at its extremes, the core—constituting representatives of all communities—has generally agreed on the ends and the means of the political game. The senior bureaucrats have largely been drawn from the same sources as the political leaders, and they seem to agree in almost all essentials concerning the conduct of government. Thus, though not permitted to become party activists, senior bureaucrats would nevertheless react to political stimuli almost the same as any other good Alliance follower. A marked deviant from the political consensus is unlikely to be found among the senior bureaucrats. In a sense this introduces a new element of ascription, but it represents a situation that could be duplicated almost anywhere else in the world today. A communist is no more likely to become a Permanent Secretary in present-day Malaya than he is to become a bureau chief in modern America.

(3) *Degree of Rationality in the Administrative Process*

Before assessing the place of rationality in Malayan administration, it might be well first to explain precisely how the term "rationality" is to be employed.[6] As used here, the measure of rationality is derived from our evaluation of the relationship between ends and means. Means and intermediate goals may be rational or irrational; ultimate goals are non-rational. If on the basis of empirical observation, experimentation, or collected information a particular means seems likely to achieve a given end, then it is rational. Ultimate goals are not amenable to rational determination, for they are after all commitments of faith, not reason. If the goal of a social system is stability, order, and social

6. The use of "rationality" here draws heavily from Joseph J. Spengler, "Theory, Ideology, Non-Economic Values, and Politico-Economic Development," in Ralph Braibanti and Joseph J. Spengler, eds., *Traditions, Values and Socio-Economic Development* (Durham, N.C.: Duke University Press, 1961), pp. 3–56.

immobility, then industrialization—from our experience thus far
—would seem to be an irrational means or an irrational intermediate goal. If the ultimate goal of the society is economic betterment or socio-economic welfare advances for the majority of the
society, then industrialization would seem to be a rational means.
Thus, in analyzing the degree of rationality in Malayan administration we must also try to discover the more general goals before
appraising ends-means relationships, but it should be pointed out
that here we are engaged in a hazardous undertaking. One may
feel with some certainty that he has grasped the general goals of
the society from a reading of the available literature of the period,
but the process must remain largely intuitive, for it is rare that
explicit statements can be discovered to support such intuitive
generalizations.

If the dominant values of pre-European society in Malaya were
stability and self-perpetuation of the ruling groups, as a reading
of the literature of the period seems to suggest, then the bureaucratic and political structure of the period could be described as
highly rational. The ascriptive nature of political recruitment,
the use of magic and ritual, and the reliance upon custom and
religion as sources of political authority virtually assured the
continuation of the society along the lines of its traditional organization.

Disruptive influences were introduced from outside Malaya in
the person of the Europeans—first the Portuguese, later the
Dutch, and finally the British. European goals and indigenous
goals did not at first coincide, for the Europeans had come to
trade, and commerce immediately sowed the seeds of change.
Moreover, as the British penetrated inland and pacified the
troubled tin mining areas, the stage was set for extensive immigration of alien groups that was further to disrupt the stability
of the social and political system. Yet a subtle but significant
change of goals was taking place on the part of both the Malays
and the British. The Malay ruling classes were learning to appreciate—and to expect—the economic wealth and the renewed
stability that the British presence had brought them, and the
British colonial administration was becoming increasingly con-

cerned about the welfare of the Sultans and their subjects. Thus, while there might initially have been a clash of goals, by the time of the Treaty of Federation of 1896, in the Federated Malay States (and perhaps somewhat later in the UMS) there was a harmonious meshing of goals and a generally rational approach toward the attainment of these ends. The major outbreaks of irrationality—in the view of British commercial interests—occurred chiefly on occasions when British colonial officers were influenced in decision-making more by their concern for the well-being of the Malays than by their interest in the economic welfare of British business. For European businessmen, this occasional confusion of goals—or what they perceived to be goals—produced irrational administrative conduct. Whether it was irrational in the view of Whitehall is a question that cannot be answered for many years.

The goals of present-day Malaya fortunately can be more readily perceived and documented. The *Second Five-Year Plan* goes to great lengths to detail the economic objectives of the nation, but in concluding that "the real challenge of the Plan is less one of raising funds than of raising and sustaining initiative, efficiency, drive, and effort," [7] the government has indicated that it is now firmly committed to social goals of change and innovation. Malaya is striving for economic betterment and increased social welfare measures for both rural and urban populations through imported methods and techniques, goals that are far removed from those of traditional and—to a less extent—even colonial Malaya.

As Professor LaPalombara has pointed out,[8] we cannot be too parochial in determining what constitutes a rational approach, for there are always limitations on what is possible in a given situation. Within the limitation of the politically possible, the bureaucracy is approaching the ends of society in a rational manner. Data collection is now far superior to that found almost anywhere else in the underdeveloped world—though it may still fall

7. Federation of Malaya, *Second Five-Year Plan, 1961–1965* (Kuala Lumpur: Government Press, 1961), p. 66.
8. *Op. cit.*, pp. 46–47.

somewhat below desired levels—financial and economic advisers are employed and their advice seems generally to be accepted, technical specialists are trained for key posts before they replace the retiring expatriates, and, in general, the senior bureaucracy is thoroughly permeated by an appreciation of the necessity of empirical observation, deliberation, and rational decision-making. Sometimes ends-means relationships are dimly perceived, and for some bureaucrats—who may unfortunately be the most vocal— they may not even be recognized, but on the whole Malayan bureaucracy today is characterized by a high degree of rationality. Political and bureaucratic leaders know where they want Malaya to go, and the bureaucracy is continually trying to find a reasonably short route to get there.

II. Bureaucracy in Transition: The Future

Many of the bureaucratic problems arising out of the transition from colonial to independent status seemed to be receding into the background by early 1961. Malayanization was no longer a seriously debated issue, proposals had been made and were being considered for tidying up many of the loose ends of administration left over from the colonial period or collected by accretion after independence, and in general the bureaucracy seemed to be settling down for the long pull of carrying out Malaya's ambitious development plans. Suddenly the picture began to assume new dimensions, and the spirit of urgency that pervaded Kuala Lumpur in 1957–58 began to return. Offices that in air-conditioned comfort had begun to fall into the unexciting routine characteristic of any mature bureaucracy suddenly began to pulsate with enthusiasm and expectation. The cause of this rash of activity was the realization that Malaya might extend its frontiers beyond the causeway to become the Federation of Malaysia—a potentially powerful state embracing Malaya, Singapore, Sarawak, North Borneo, and, it was hoped, Brunei.

On May 27, 1961, Tengku Abdul Rahman, Prime Minister of Malaya, in an address before a press luncheon in Singapore suggested that a new Federation of Malaysia was both desirable and possible.[9] Though this address was presented by the Prime Minister in a typically offhand manner, the response was spontaneous and enthusiastic in Malaya, while in the other territories it was apparent that many leaders were receptive to the idea if not genuinely enthusiastic. The Tengku traveled to London in October, a Commission of Enquiry was created following these discussions,[10] and the Commission's Report was submitted to the British and Malayan governments on June 21, 1962.[11] Further talks were held in London on the basis of the *Report,* an Intergovernmental Working Committee was appointed to formulate constitutional proposals, and the *Report* of this Committee was published in February, 1963.[12] The proposed constitution, based on the existing Malayan Constitution, was submitted for ratification to each of the legislatures, accepted with minor amendments, and the Federation of Malaysia came into existence on September 16, 1963.[13]

Malaysian bureaucracy must now attack new and expanded political and economic goals with proportionately less manpower and financial resources than it enjoyed before the creation of the larger Federation. Moreover, the newly amalgamated bureaucracy has found itself joined but not integrated, and this problem of integration is likely to be one that will attract the attention of public administration specialists for many years to come. In internal administration Malaya must now resolve at least four basic problems, each of which was faced and temporarily or permanently resolved previously in Malaya, though now some of the solutions may not be applicable in the new Federation.

9. For a summary of these remarks, see *Straits Times* (Singapore and Kuala Lumpur), May 28, 1961, p. 1.
10. Cmnd. 1563 (1961).
11. Great Britain and Federation of Malaya, Commission of Enquiry, North Borneo and Sarawak, 1962 (Lord Cobbold, Chairman), *Report* (Kuala Lumpur: Government Press, 1962). (The *Report* was published simultaneously in London, Kuala Lumpur, and Kuching.)
12. Great Britain, *Malaysia: Report of the Inter-Governmental Committee, 1962* (London: HMSO, 1963) [Cmnd. 1954].
13. The short but complex history of the creation of Malaysia has been presented here only in the briefest outline. There is now a rapidly growing body of literature concerning the emergence of the Federation.

(1) *Nationalization of the Colonial Services*

Malayanization in the Peninsula was, within political limitations, rational, efficient, and effective. Now it must be undertaken again. Singapore has had its own scheme for replacing expatriates, and, while it will probably be accelerated, there is no reason for suspecting any genuine difficulties in the years ahead. Plans for the Borneanization of the services in Sarawak and North Borneo, which were drawn almost verbatim from the Malayan scheme, were written into the Lansdowne Committee *Report*. The mechanics of the plan should provide little difficulty; expatriate officers expect to be replaced by local recruits, and a valuable corpus of precedents is available in the Malayan experience to draw upon. The major obstacle will be the availability of high-level manpower (again to borrow the term from Nigeria's Ashby Commission *Report*). Education, particularly secondary and post-secondary education, does not have the history in the Bornean territories that it has in Singapore and Malaya, and thus there is not a ready reservoir of talent to send off to Singapore, Malaya, Australia, or Great Britain for advanced training, as was done under the Malayanization scheme. There is always the danger that political necessity may dictate an accelerated program of replacement that is unrealistic in the context of the Bornean environment. The answer may lie in transferring some scarce but nevertheless available technical officers from Singapore and Malaya to take over from retiring expatriates at least until local officers become available; however, as it will be pointed out later, political realities make this solution less attractive than it at first appears.

(2) *Standardization of Salaries and Classifications of Posts*

The work that the Trusted, Benham, Willan, and Himsworth Committees did in restructuring Malayan bureaucracy will now have to be done again for Malaysian bureaucracy. Bureaucratic organization in the Peninsula—still far from the ideal posited by many observers—now seems rationally structured and neat compared with Malaysian bureaucracy as a whole. Bureaucratic structures and procedures in Singapore and Malaya, always considered more or less distinct depending upon the period, had increasingly taken on separate existences from the time the island was administratively divorced from the peninsula after World War II. Now the trend must be reversed, and to unify the structures will require many compromises on the part of both in view of the inconsistent classifications of posts and related salaries in the two areas. Unification, or standardization, between Singapore and Malaya will undoubtedly be troublesome, but the problems will probably not be so formidable as will be the integration of the Bornean bureaucracies.

In each of the Bornean territories a unique bureaucratic history has affected the structure and operation of the present-day system. Although all three territories enjoyed British protection after 1888, until the interruption of the Japanese occupation North Borneo was administered by personnel of the North Borneo (Chartered) Company Limited, Sarawak by a personal and dedicated staff employed by the Brookes (the White Rajahs of Sarawak), and Brunei by the Sultan's civil service, which was composed of expatriates, Malay royalty, palace favorites, and, later, Malay officers borrowed from the Federation of Malaya. There have been many administrative reforms tending toward standardization since 1946, particularly in Sarawak and North Borneo, but the influences of these differing experiences are still much in evidence.

It will be necessary eventually to bring some order out of the present chaotic structuring of Malaysian bureaucracy, for the efficient operation of the machine as well as for the perhaps more important but less tangible benefits it will bring in the process of national integration. The problems, however, are formidable, and the tasks will be herculean.

(3) *Standardization of the Administrative Services*

The functional equivalent of the Malayan Civil Service exists in each of the territories outside the peninsula, but none of these services enjoy the traditions and the prestige of the MCS. Probably the MCS cannot be successfully exported outside Malaya, however, for to do so might occasion considerable resentment and in the end could be more detrimental than beneficial. The Malay–non-Malay quota arrangement was thoroughly distasteful to Sarawak and North Borneo and beyond consideration in Singapore. In Sarawak and North Borneo there was considerable interest in equating "Malay" with "native" for purposes of recruitment; the Constitution provides an entering wedge for implementing such an equation.[14] Colonial authorities before independence, however, repeatedly voiced assurances to the Chinese residents that such discrimination in the bureaucracy would not be permitted, and there is still considerable popular sentiment against the imposition of quotas in the administrative services. It seems highly desirable that there should be a standardization if not an actual unification of the various territorial administrative services, but at least in the foreseeable future it is likely that social and political realities will provide insurmountable obstacles to any genuine reorganization.

(4) *The Creation of a Common Establishment*

For political as well as administrative reasons, a long-range goal of Malaysian bureaucracy is likely to be the creation of a common establishment, which would permit all Malaysian officers to be transferred throughout the five territories. The problem is of essentially the same nature—though on a larger scale and complicated by regional and communal differences—as that faced by the Federated Malay States and the Unfederated Malay States a quarter-century after the implementation of the Treaty of Federation of 1896. The Malayan Establishment Office was created in 1934 to rationalize the confused practices of lending and borrowing officers, and the logical answer might now seem to be the establishment of a Malaysian establishment office.

14. Based on the most recent statistics available (1957 in the case of Malaya and Singapore; 1960 for the Bornean territories), Sarawak's population has about 51 per cent natives and 31 per cent Chinese; in North Borneo the figures are 71 per cent and 23 per cent. The term "native" is used officially to describe the various tribes of Borneo, the major ones being the Iban in Sarawak and the Dusun in North Borneo.

However neat and attractive this solution might seem, it is nevertheless apparent that it is likely to be many years before Malaysian officers can expect to be transferred freely throughout the entire area. The mere mechanics of the problem, which have already been discussed briefly, are enough to discourage most transfers. Moreover, until a more general political consensus emerges throughout Malaysia it is improbable that anything but selected and limited transfers will be possible. The only territories currently in a position to act as donors are Malaya and Singapore, and it seems likely that any move on their part to assign senior officers to the Bornean territories in sizeable numbers will not be received with much enthusiasm. Malaysia was created with assurances to the Bornean territories that it constituted neither Malay imperialism nor a means of relieving Singapore's overcrowded conditions and persisting unemployment. The transfer of either community to Borneo in substantial numbers could be interpreted as a breach of faith. As such, it might provide fuel for an anti-Malaysian opposition group that is almost certain to continue smoldering within Borneo for some time to come.

III. Bureaucracy in Transition: A Summation

As this and previous chapters have pointed out, numerous problems face both the present and future bureaucracies, many relatively minor but some of a more formidable nature. Conceding that there are many more hurdles in the path of modernization—any one or combination of which could be disastrous in a given environment—it must still be accepted that Malaya has faced one of its most difficult obstacles and has successfully surmounted it. Malaya has imported a modern system of administration, *it* has largely replaced the foreigners with indigenous officers from another cultural tradition, and the system is still working—not always precisely as it did in the colonial environment, but it is effectively serving the present ends of the society. This, after all, is high praise, for it is the *raison d'être* of bureaucracy.

Appendixes

Appendix A

Questionnaire for Writers Receiving Appointments
in the Service of the East India Company *

Question 1. Produce the Declaration from your Parent or next of kin that your appointment was gratuitously made.

Question 2. Have you any reason to doubt the correctness or accuracy of that document?

Question 3. What was the situation, Profession, and Residence of your Parents or next of kin?

Question 4. Are any of them acquainted with said Director who recommended you for your appointment? Which of them?

Question 5. How long have you been acquainted with said Director?

Question 6. By whom were you recommended to the Director presenting you for this appointment?

Question 7. Do you believe that any person has received or is to receive any pecuniary consideration or anything convertible in any mode into pecuniary benefit on account of your appointment?

Question 8. Are you aware that if your appointment shall appear to have been obtained through corrupt or other improper means it will render you ineligible to receive any appointment whatever in the Company Service?

* This form is extracted, with answers of the individual servant omitted, from *Straits Settlements Records*, Vol. A47, *Penang: Consultations, 1827*, letter from London dated October 18, 1826, presented to Council, June 12, 1827, pp. 6, 7.

Appendix B

Agreements for the Constitution of a
Federation Establishment

I. *Agreement of 1955*

AGREEMENT dated the 1st day of January, 1955, and made between the Governments of the Federation of Malaya, of the States of Johore, Kedah, Kelantan, Negri Sembilan, Pahang, Perak, Perlis, Selangor and Trengganu and of the Settlements of Penang and Malacca.

WHEREAS certain officers by the conditions of their employment are liable to serve in appropriate offices under more than one of the Governments which are parties to this Agreement:

AND WHEREAS it is desirable that suitable arrangements shall be made for the appointment, posting, promotion and control of such officers.

NOW IT IS HEREBY AGREED as follows:

1. This Agreement shall come into operation on the first day of January, 1955.

2. There shall be constituted a Federation Establishment consisting of officers whose conditions of employment involve a liability to serve in appropriate offices under more than one of the Governments which are parties to this Agreement.

3. Each of the said Governments hereby undertakes to accept and employ officers who have been appointed to the Federation Establishment in all the offices set out in the Schedule to this Agreement * (hereinafter referred to as "the scheduled offices") and in default to pay all expenses resulting from such default.

4. The Schedule may be altered by way of addition to or deletion from the list of offices therein set out at the instance of the Government concerned and with the approval of the High Commissioner:

Provided that where any office is deleted from the Schedule, the Government at whose instance such deletion was made shall, unless due notice is given, be responsible for any expenses consequent upon the deletion of such office.

5. The Federation Establishment shall be administered by the Chief

* The Schedule to the Agreement has not been included in this appendix.

Secretary in accordance with the instructions of the High Commissioner.

6. Appointments to the Federation Establishment shall be made by the High Commissioner on the advice of the Public Service Commission or such other body (if any) as may be appointed by the High Commissioner for that purpose.

7. Officers after appointment to the Federation Establishment shall be posted for duty in the scheduled offices in accordance with the instructions of the High Commissioner and after, in each case, consultation with the Government of the State or Settlement concerned.

8. There shall be created a Federation Establishment Board which shall consist of the Chief Secretary, who shall be Chairman, two State Secretaries, to be nominated by the Conference of Rulers, and the Resident Commissioner, Penang.

9. Any question relating to the administration of the Federation Establishment may be considered by the Board, and it shall be the duty of the Board to advise the High Commissioner with respect thereto.

II. *Agreement of 1957*

AGREEMENT dated the 13th day of August, 1957, and made between the Governments of the Federation of Malaya, of the States of Johore, Kedah, Kelantan, Negri Sembilan, Pahang, Perak, Perlis, Selangor, and Trengganu and of the Settlements of Penang and Malacca.

WHEREAS certain officers by the conditions of their employment are liable to serve in appropriate offices under more than one of the Governments which are parties to this Agreement:

AND WHEREAS, it is desirable that suitable arrangements shall be made for the appointment, posting, promotion and control of such officers.

NOW IT IS HEREBY AGREED as follows:

1. This Agreement shall come into operation on the 13th day of August, 1957.

2. There shall be constituted a Federation Establishment consisting of officers whose conditions of employment involve a liability to serve in appropriate offices under more than one of the Governments which are parties to this Agreement.

3. Each of the said Governments hereby undertakes to accept and employ officers who have been appointed to the Federation Establishment in all the offices set out in the Schedule to this Agreement *

* The Schedule to the Agreement has not been included.

(hereinafter referred to as "the scheduled offices") and in default to pay all expenses resulting from such default.

4. This Schedule may be altered by way of addition to or deletion from the list of offices therein set out at the instance of the Government concerned and with the approval of the Yang di-Pertuan Agong.

Provided that where any office is deleted from the Schedule, the Government at whose instance such deletion was made shall, unless due notice is given, be responsible for any expenses consequent upon the deletion of such office.

5. Subject to the provisions of Part X of the Constitution the Federation Establishment shall be administered by the Principal Establishment Officer.

6. Subject to the provisions of Article 144 of the Constitution officers on the Federation Establishment shall be posted for duty in the scheduled offices by the Principal Establishment Officer, or by the appropriate Head of Department under the general authority of the Public Services Commission after, in each case, consultation with the Government of the State concerned.

Appendix C

Constitution of the Federation of Malaya, Part X:
The Public Services

132. (1) For the purposes of this Constitution, the public services are—

(a) the armed forces;
(b) the judicial and legal service;
(c) the general public service of the Federation;
(d) the police force;
(e) the railway service;
(f) the joint public services mentioned in Article 133; and
(g) the public service of each State.

(2) Except as otherwise expressly provided by this Constitution, the qualifications for appointment and conditions of service of persons in the public services other than those mentioned in paragraph (g) of Clause (1) may be regulated by federal law and, subject to the provisions of any such law, by the Yang di-Pertuan Agong; and the qualifications for appointment and conditions of service of persons in the public service of any State may be regulated by State law and, subject to the provisions of any such law, by the Ruler or Governor of that State.

(2A) Except as expressly provided by this Constitution, every person who is a member of any of the services mentioned in paragraphs (a), (b), (c), (d), (e) and (f) of Clause (1) holds office during the pleasure of the Yang di-Pertuan Agong, and, except as expressly provided by the Constitution of the State, every person who is a member of the public service of a State holds office during the pleasure of the Ruler or Governor.

(3) Subject to Clause (4), references to persons in the public service or to members of any of the public services do not include references to the following, that is to say,—

(a) any Minister or Assistant Minister of the Federation and the Chief Minister or any other member of the Executive Council of a State;

(b) a member of either House of Parliament or of the Legislative Assembly of a State;

(c) the Clerk to either House of Parliament and any member of the staff of Parliament;

(d) unless he has been appointed from among the members of the judicial and legal service or of the public service of his State, the legal adviser of any State;

(e) a member of the personal staff of the Yang di-Pertuan Agong or of a Ruler or Governor;

(f) persons holding such diplomatic posts in the general public service of the Federation as the Yang di-Pertuan Agong may by order prescribe;

nor to a member of any Commission or Council established by this Constitution, except that if he is a member of any of the public services in some other capacity, the said references include references to him in that capacity.

(4) Clause (3) does not restrict the application of Articles 136 and 147.

133. (1) Joint services, common to the Federation and one or more of the States or, at the request of the States concerned, to two or more States, may be established by federal law.

(2) Where a member of any of the public services is employed—

(a) partly for federal purposes and partly for State purposes, or

(b) for the purposes of two or more States,

the proportion, if any, of his remuneration payable by the Federation and the State or States concerned or, as the case may be, by each of the States concerned, shall, subject to federal law, be determined by agreement or, in default of agreement, by the Commission whose jurisdiction extends to him.

134. (1) The Federation may, at the request of a State, second any member of any of the services mentioned in paragraph (a), (b), (c), (d) or (f) of Clause (1) of Article 132 to the service of that State; and a State may at the request of the Federation or of another State second any member of its own public service to the service of the Federation or, as the case may be, of that other State.

(2) A person seconded under this Article shall remain a member of the service to which he belongs, but his remuneration shall be paid by the State to whose service he is seconded or, if he is seconded to the service of the Federation, by the Federation.

135. (1) No member of any of the services mentioned in paragraphs (b) to (g) of Clause (1) of Article 132 shall be dismissed or reduced in rank by an authority subordinate to that which, at the time of the dismissal or reduction, has power to appoint a member of that service of equal rank.

(a) a member of any of the public services;

(b) an officer or employee of any local authority or of a body corporate or authority established by law for public purposes;

(c) a member of a trade union or of a body or association affiliated to a trade union.

(3) Clause (2) does not apply to ex officio members; and a member of any of the public services may be appointed to be and remain chairman or deputy chairman and, if he is on leave prior to retirement, he may be appointed to be another member, of any of the said Commissions.

(4) Where, during any period, a member of any of the said Commissions has been granted leave of absence by the Yang di-Pertuan Agong or is unable, owing to his absence from the Federation, illness or any other cause, to discharge his functions as a member, then

(a) if he is an appointed member, the Yang di-Pertuan Agong may appoint to exercise his functions during that period any person who would be qualified to be appointed in his place, and the appointment of such a person shall be made in the same manner as that of the member whose functions he is to exercise;

(b) if he is an ex officio member, any person authorised under federal law to perform the functions of his office may during that period perform also his functions as a member of the Commission.

(5) A Commission to which this Part applies may act notwithstanding a vacancy in its membership, and no proceedings of such a Commission shall be invalidated by reason only that some person not entitled thereto has taken part in them.

(6) Before exercising his functions as a member of any of the said Commissions or under Clause (4) any person other than an ex officio member shall take and subscribe before a judge of the Supreme Court the oath of office and allegiance set out in the Sixth Schedule.

143. (1) A member of a Commission to which this Part applies, other than an ex officio member—

(a) shall be appointed for a term of five years or, if the Yang di-Pertuan Agong, acting in his discretion but after considering the advice of the Prime Minister, in a particular case so determines, for such shorter term as he may so determine;

(b) may, unless disqualified, be re-appointed from time to time; and

(c) may at any time resign his office but shall not be removed from office except on the like grounds and in the like manner as a judge of the Supreme Court.

(2) Parliament shall by law provide for the remuneration of any member of the said Commission other than a member for whose remuneration as holder of any other office provision is made by federal law; and the remuneration so provided shall be charged on the Consolidated Fund.

(3) The remuneration and other terms of office of a member of a Commission to which this Part applies shall not be altered to his disadvantage after his appointment.

144. (1) Subject to the provisions of any existing law and to the provisions of this Constitution, it shall be the duty of a Commission to which this Part applies to appoint, confirm, emplace on the permanent or pensionable establishment, promote, transfer and exercise disciplinary control over members of the service or services to which its jurisdiction extends.

(2) Federal law may provide for the exercise of other functions by any such Commission.

(3) The Yang di-Pertuan Agong may designate as special posts any post held by the head or deputy head of a department or by an officer who in his opinion is of similar status and the appointment to any post so designated shall not be made in accordance with Clause (1) but shall be made by the Yang di-Pertuan Agong on the recommendation of the Commission whose jurisdiction extends to the service in which the post is held.

(4) The Ruler or Governor of a State may designate as special posts any posts in the public service of his State held by the head or deputy head of a department or by an officer who in his opinion is of similar status; and the appointment to any post so designated shall not be made in accordance with Clause (1) but shall be made by the Ruler or Governor on the recommendation of the Public Services Commission (or, if there is in the State of any Ruler a Commission of corresponding status and jurisdiction, on the recommendation of that Commission).

(5) Before acting, in accordance with Clause (3) or (4), on the recommendation of the Commission therein mentioned—

(a) the Yang di-Pertuan Agong shall consider the advice of the Prime Minister; and

(b) the Ruler or Governor shall consider the advice of the Chief Minister of his State,

and may once refer the recommendation back to the Commission in order that it may be reconsidered.

(5A) Federal law and, subject to the provisions of any such law, regulations made by the Yang di-Pertuan Agong may, notwithstanding the provisions of Clause (1) of Article 135, provide for the exercise by any officer in a service to which the jurisdiction of a Commission to which this Part applies extends, or by any board of such officers, of any of the functions of the Commission under Clause (1):

Provided that—

(a) no such law or regulation may provide for the exercise by any such officer or board of officers of any power of first appointment to the permanent or pensionable establishment, or to any power of promotion (other than promotion to an acting appointment); and

(b) any person aggrieved by the exercise by any such officer or board of officers of any power of disciplinary control may appeal to the Commission within such time and in such manner as may be prescribed by any such law or regulations, and the Commission may make such order thereon as it may consider just.

(6) A Commission to which this Part applies may delegate to any officer in a service to which its jurisdiction extends, or to any board of such officers appointed by it, any of its functions under Clause (1) in respect of any grade of service, and that officer or board shall exercise those functions under the direction and the control of the Commission.

(7) In this Article "transfer" does not include transfer without change of rank within a department of government.

(8) A Commission to which this Part applies may, subject to the provisions of this Constitution and of federal law, make rules regulating its procedure and specifying the number of its members which are to constitute a quorum.

145. (1) The Yang di-Pertuan Agong shall, on the advice of the Prime Minister, appoint a person who is qualified to be a judge of the Supreme Court to be the Attorney General for the Federation.

(2) It shall be the duty of the Attorney General to advise the Yang di-Pertuan Agong or the Cabinet or any Minister upon such legal matters, and to perform such other duties of a legal character, as may from time to time be referred or assigned to him by the Yang di-Pertuan Agong or the Cabinet, and to discharge the functions conferred on him by or under this Constitution or any other written law.

(3) The Attorney General shall have power, exercisable at his discretion, to institute, conduct or discontinue any proceedings for an offence, other than proceedings before a Muslim court or a court-martial.

(4) In the performance of his duties the Attorney General shall have the right of audience in, and shall take precedence over any

other person appearing before, any court or tribunal in the Federation.

(5) Subject to Clause (6), the Attorney General shall hold office during the pleasure of the Yang di-Pertuan Agong and may at any time resign his office and, unless he is a member of the Cabinet, shall receive such remuneration as the Yang di-Pertuan Agong may determine.

(6) The person holding the office of Attorney General immediately prior to the coming into operation of this Article shall continue to hold the office on terms and conditions not less favourable than those applicable to him immediately before such coming into operation and shall not be removed from office except on the like grounds and in the like manner as a judge of the Supreme Court.

146. (1) Each of the Commissions to which this Part applies shall make an annual report on its activities to the Yang di-Pertuan Agong and copies of those reports shall be laid before both Houses of Parliament.

(2) The Public Services Commission shall send a copy of every report made under this Article to the Ruler or Governor of each State to members of whose public service their jurisdiction extends, and the Ruler or Governor shall lay it before the Legislative Assembly.

147. (1) The law applicable to any pension, gratuity or other like allowance (in this Article referred to as an "award") granted to a member of any of the public services, or to his widow, children, dependent or personal representatives, shall be that in force on the relevant day or any later law not less favourable to the person to whom the award is made.

(2) For the purposes of this Article the relevant day is—

    (a) in relation to an award made before Merdeka Day, the date on which the award was made;

    (b) in relation to an award made after Merdeka Day to or in respect of any person who was a member of any of the public services before Merdeka Day, the thirtieth day of August, nineteen hundred and fifty-seven;

    (c) in relation to an award made to or in respect of any person who first became a member of any of the public services on or after Merdeka Day, the date on which he first became such a member.

(3) For the purposes of this Article, where the law applicable to an award depends on the option of the person to whom it is made, the law for which he opts shall be taken to be more favourable to him than any other law for which he might have opted.

148. (1) References in this Constitution to a Commission to which

this Part applies are, unless the context otherwise requires, references to any of the Commissions established under Articles 139 to 141.

(2) In this Part "ex officio member" includes a Minister and a judge of the Supreme Court.

Selected Bibliography

A Selected Bibliography of Public Documents
Relating to Malayan Bureaucracy

I. Malaya

A. *Indian Archive Records* (*Microfilm*)

INDIAN NATIONAL ARCHIVES. *Manuscripts Relating to the Straits Settlements*. New Delhi: National Archives of India, 1955. Reel 1. "Correspondence with the Resident at Singapore." Foreign Miscellaneous Series 250, 251.

———. ———. ———. ———. "Papers Related to Prince of Wales Island." Home Miscellaneous Series 213.

———. ———. ———. ———. Miscellaneous Correspondence with Malacca, 1811–1916. Home Miscellaneous Series 353.

———. ———. ———. Reels 2–5. "Public Department Original Consultations, 1786–1795."

———. ———. ———. Reels 5, 6. "Prince of Wales Island, Proceedings of the Secret and Political Departments, 1806–1812." Series 116–118.

———. ———. ———. Reels 6–8. "Malacca Proceedings, 1852–1860."

———. ———. ———. Reels 8–13. "Narrative of Abstracts of the Proceedings of the Government of the Straits Settlements in the Various Departments, 1855–1859." Home Miscellaneous Series 525–541.

———. ———. ———. Reels 13, 14. "Public Department Proceedings Relative to Prince of Wales Island." Series 199–201.

B. *Raffles National Archive Records*

STRAITS SETTLEMENTS RECORDS. Singapore: Raffles National Library. Vol. A3. *Penang: Consultations, 1807.*

———. ———. Vol. A24. *Penang: Consultations, 1825–1826.*

———. ———. Vol. A26. *Penang: Consultations, 1826.*

———. ———. Vol. A47. *Penang: Consultations, 1827.*

———. ———. Vol. A57. *Penang: Consultations, 1828.*

———. ———. Vol. A64. *Penang: Consultations, 1829.*

———. ———. Vol. A65. *Penang: Consultations, 1829.*

————. ————. Vol. B1. *Penang: Letters to London, 1805–1806.*

————. ————. Vol. B3. *Penang: Letters to London, 1813–1814.*

————. ————. Vol. C2. *Penang: Letters from London, 1815–1816.*

————. ————. Vol. C6. *Penang: Letters from London, 1828–1829.*

————. ————. Vol. H11. *Penang: Letters and Orders in Council, 1824.*

————. ————. Vol. I28. *Penang: Miscellaneous Letters (Out). 1825–1826.*

————. ————. Vol. 139. *Penang: Miscellaneous Letters (In).*

————. ————. Vol. L17. *Raffles Letters to Singapore, 1823.*

————. ————. Vol. R33. *Letters to Bengal, 1858.*

————. ————. Vol. R38. *Governor's Letters to Bengal 1860–1861.*

————. ————. Vol. S26. *Governor's Letters from Bengal, 1858.*

————. ————. Vol. S28. *Governor's Letters from India, 1860.*

C. Reports

CONGRESS OF UNIONS OF EMPLOYEES OF THE PUBLIC AND CIVIL SERVICES (CUEPACS), *Annual Report and Statement of Accounts, 1959–60.* Kuala Lumpur: The Economy Printers, Ltd., 1960.

FEDERATED MALAY STATES. BUCKNILL, SIR JOHN A. S. *Report of the Committee Appointed by His Excellency the Governor of the Straits Settlements and the High Commissioner of the Federated Malay States.* London: His Majesty's Stationery Office, 1919.

FEDERATED MALAY STATES AND COLONY OF SINGAPORE. MACGREGOR, A. D. A. *Report of the Committee on Temporary Allowances.* Singapore: Government Printing Office, 1937.

Federation of Malaya. Atkinson, G. A. *Report on the Housing for Division I Government Officers in the Federation of Malaya.* Kuala Lumpur: Government Press, 1952.

————. ————. *Report on Housing for Government Officers in Division II and Lower Divisions, the Federation of Malaya.* Kuala Lumpur: Government Press, 1953.

————. Benham, F. C. *Report of the Special Committee on Salaries in the Federation of Malaya.* Kuala Lumpur: Government Press, 1950.

————. Blacker, M. H. *Report on Post-Entry Training in Government Service.* Kuala Lumpur: mimeographed, 1952.

————. Haimes, W. J. *Report to His Excellency the Officer Administering the Government, Sir Donald MacGillivray.* Kuala Lumpur: mimeographed, 1953.

————. *Malayanization of the Public Service: A Statement of Policy.* Kuala Lumpur: Government Press, 1956.

————. *The 1957 Census, a Preliminary Report Based on First-Count Totals.* Kuala Lumpur: Government Press, 1957.

————. *Report of the Activities of the Judicial and Legal Service Commission for the Years Ending 31st December 1957 and 1958*. Kuala Lumpur: Government Press, 1960.

————. *Report of the Commission to Enquire into Matters Affecting the Integrity of the Public Services, 1955*. Kuala Lumpur: Government Press, 1955.

————. *Report of the Committee on the Malayanization of the Government Service*. Kuala Lumpur: Government Press, 1954.

————. *Report of the Committee on the Malayanization of the Public Service*. Kuala Lumpur: Government Press, 1956.

————. *Report of the Land Administration Commission*. Kuala Lumpur: Government Press, 1958.

————. *Report of the Police Service Commission for the Years Ending 31st December 1957 and 1958*. Kuala Lumpur: Government Press, 1960.

————. *Report of the Public Services Commission for the Years 1957 and 1958*. Kuala Lumpur: Government Press, 1960.

————. *Salaries in the Public Service*. Kuala Lumpur: Government Press, 1955.

————. Willan, Harold. *Report of the Professional Officers' Committee*. Kuala Lumpur: Government Press, 1950.

————. Federation Establishment Office. Whitley Council (Divisions I–IV). *First Bulletin*. Kuala Lumpur: Economy Printers, Ltd., 1954.

————. ————. ————. *Second Bulletin*. Alor Star: Kedah Government Press, 1955.

————. ————. ————. *Third Bulletin*. Alor Star: Kedah Government Press, 1957.

————. ————. ————. *Fourth Bulletin*. Alor Star: Kedah Government Press, 1958.

————. ————. ————. *Fifth Bulletin*. Alor Star: Kedah Government Press, 1958.

————. ————. ————. *Sixth Bulletin*. Alor Star: Kedah Government Press, 1959.

————. ————. ————. *Seventh Bulletin*. Alor Star: Kedah Government Press, 1960.

————. ————. ————. *Eighth Bulletin*. Alor Star: Kedah Government Press, 1961.

————. ————. ————. *Ninth Bulletin*. Alor Star: Kedah Government Press, 1962.

————. Public Service Appointments and Promotions Board. *Report for the Period June to December, 1954*. Kuala Lumpur: typescript, 1955.

——. ——. *Report for the Year 1955.* Kuala Lumpur: mimeographed, 1956.

——. ——. *Report for the Year Ending 31st December 1956.* Kuala Lumpur: mimeographed, 1957.

——. Whitley Council (Divisions I–IV). Staff Side. *Second Annual Report.* Kuala Lumpur: Economy Printers, Ltd., 1955.

——. ——. ——. *Third Annual Report.* Kuala Lumpur: Khee Meng Press, 1956.

——. ——. ——. *Fourth Annual Report.* Kuala Lumpur: Khee Meng Press, 1957.

——. ——. ——. *Fifth Annual Report.* Kuala Lumpur: Khee Meng Press, 1958.

——. ——. ——. *Sixth Annual Report.* Kuala Lumpur: Khee Meng Press, 1959.

——. ——. ——. *Seventh Annual Report.* Kuala Lumpur: The Commercial Press Ltd., 1960.

——. ——. ——. *Eighth Annual Report.* Kuala Lumpur: Loyal Press, 1961.

FEDERATION OF MALAYA AND COLONY OF SINGAPORE. COWGILL, J. V. *Report on Revision of Salaries in the Public Services of the Federation of Malaya and the Colony of Singapore.* Kuala Lumpur: Government Press, 1949.

——. Himsworth, E. *Report of the Committee on the Examination of the Superscale Salaries of Division I of the Public Services of the Federation of Malaya and the Colony of Singapore.* Kuala Lumpur: Government Press, 1954.

——. Joint Committee on Cost of Living Allowances. *Report.* Kuala Lumpur: Government Press, 1948.

MALAYAN UNION. PYKE, C. J. *Report of the Wages and Cost of Living Committee.* Kuala Lumpur: Government Press, 1946.

MALAYAN UNION AND SINGAPORE. TRUSTED, SIR HARRY. *Report of the Public Services Salaries Commission of Malaya, 1947.* Kuala Lumpur: Government Press, 1947.

D. *Circulars*

FEDERATION OF MALAYA. *Federation Establishment Office Circular.* No. 5 of 1955. "Superscale Salary Schemes." Kuala Lumpur: Government Press, 1955.

——. ——. No. 8 of 1955. "Consolidation of a Further Part of Cost of Living Allowance with Basic Salary." Kuala Lumpur: Government Press, 1955.

——. ——. No. 9 of 1955. "Postings and Withdrawals of Officers to and from States." Kuala Lumpur: Government Press, 1955.

———. ———. No. 18 of 1955. "Revision of Titles of Superscale Grades in Division I." Kuala Lumpur: Government Press, 1955.

———. ———. No. 4 of 1956. "Revision of Clerical Services' Salaries." Kuala Lumpur: Government Press, 1956.

———. ———. No. 14 of 1956. "Abolition of Classes within the M.C.S. Timescale." Kuala Lumpur: Government Press, 1956.

———. ———. No. 21 of 1956. "Pension Allowances, as Amended by F. E. O. Letter 323/IV Dated October 8, 1956." Kuala Lumpur: Government Press, 1956.

———. ———. No. 6 of 1957. Untitled. Kuala Lumpur: Government Press, 1957.

———. General Circular. No. 1 of 1951. "Circulars." Kuala Lumpur: Government Press, 1951.

———. ———. No. 7 of 1954. "The Federation Establishment Office." Kuala Lumpur: Government Press, 1954.

———. ———. No. 2 of 1956. "The Public Services Commission, the Judicial and Legal Service Commission and the Police Service Commission." Kuala Lumpur: Government Press, 1956.

———. ———. No. 1 of 1957. "Circulars." Kuala Lumpur: Government Press, 1957.

———. ———. No. 4 of 1957. "The Special Committees of the Cabinet." Kuala Lumpur: Government Press, 1957.

———. ———. No. 2 of 1958. "Amendments to *General Circular* No. 4 of 1957." Kuala Lumpur: Government Press, 1958.

———. ———. No. 4 of 1959. "Organization within Ministries." Kuala Lumpur: Government Press, 1959.

———. Service Circular. No. 22 of 1951. "The Establishments Division." Kuala Lumpur: Government Press, 1951.

———. ———. No. 4 of 1952. "Authority for Approval of Appointments or Promotions to Division I and Division II Federal Posts Contained in the Federation of Malaya Schemes of Service." Kuala Lumpur: Government Press, 1952.

———. ———. No. 2 of 1957. "Cost of Living Allowances and Expatriation Allowances to Married and Divorced Officers." Kuala Lumpur: Government Press, 1957.

———. ———. No. 15 of 1958. "Public Holidays and Unrecorded Leave for Officers in Divisions I–IV." Kuala Lumpur: Government Press, 1958.

———. ———. No. 4 of 1959. "Re-employment of Pensioners." Kuala Lumpur: Government Press, 1959.

———. ———. No. 6 of 1959. "Malay Munshi Allowance." Kuala Lumpur: Government Press, 1959.

———. ———. No. 8 of 1959. "Retiring Allowance and Gratuity Norms." Kuala Lumpur: Government Press, 1959.

————. ————. No. 9 of 1959. "Gratuities Payable Under Section 17 (1) of the Pensions Ordinance 1951 to the Dependents of Government Officers Who Die in the Service, or, in the Absence of Any Dependents, to the Legal Personal Representative." Kuala Lumpur: Government Press, 1959.

————. ————. No. 10 of 1959. "Agreements for Scholarships and Study Leave Awards." Kuala Lumpur: Government Press, 1959.

————. ————. No. 1 of 1960. "Free Water, Conservancy and Scavenging." Kuala Lumpur: Government Press, 1960.

————. ————. No. 2 of 1960. "Retiring Age of Women." Kuala Lumpur: Government Press, 1960.

————. ————. No. 9 of 1960. "Applications for Fellowships, Scholarships and Training Awards Offered by Bodies other than the Federation Government." Kuala Lumpur: mimeographed, 1960.

————. *Treasury Circular.* No. 8 of 1957. "Advance to Officers for the Purchase of Motor Vehicles." Kuala Lumpur: Government Press, 1957.

————. ————. No. 1 of 1958. "Action to Be Taken on Reports Issued by the Organization and Methods Division." Kuala Lumpur: Government Press, 1958.

————. ————. No. 5 of 1958. "Outfit Allowance for Duty Overseas." Kuala Lumpur: Government Press, 1958.

————. ————. No. 7 of 1958. "Allowances Payable to Government Officers for Attendance in Court." Kuala Lumpur: Government Press, 1958.

————. *Federal Secretariat Circular.* No. 3 of 1949. Untitled. Kuala Lumpur: mimeographed, 1949.

————. ————. No. 13 of 1950. Untitled. Kuala Lumpur: Government Press, 1950.

————. *F. E. O. Circular Letter.* No. 59 of 1956. F. E. O. 3794/24. Untitled. Kuala Lumpur: typescript, 1956.

————. ————. F. E. O. 5694/29. "Revision of Syllabus for the M. C. S. Law Examination." Kuala Lumpur: typescript, 1958.

————. *F. E. O. Conference Series 1180.* Untitled. Kuala Lumpur: typescript, 1957.

————. *F. E. O. 4910.* Untitled. Kuala Lumper: typescript, 1958.

————. *F. E. O. 4910/51.* Untitled. Kuala Lumpur: typescript, 1959.

————. *Treasury Circular Letter.* Try. (Est.) 1556/3. Untitled. Kuala Lumpur: typescript, 1953.

E. *Legislative Papers and Debates*

FEDERATED MALAY STATES. *Federal Council Proceedings.* Kuala Lumpur: Government Press, 1938.

FEDERATION OF MALAYA. FEDERAL LEGISLATIVE COUNCIL. Third Session. *Minutes and Council Papers.* Kuala Lumpur: Government Press, 1954. No. 7 of 1950. "Expatriation Pay."

——. ——. Fourth Session. *Minutes and Council Papers.* Kuala Lumpur: Government Press, 1952. No. 16 of 1951. "Report of the Joint Committee on Cost of Living Allowances."

——. ——. Fifth Session. *Minutes and Council Papers.* Kuala Lumpur: Government Press, 1954. No. 48 of 1952. "Negotiations with Government Staff Unions and Associations."

——. ——. Seventh Session. *Minutes and Council Papers.* Kuala Lumpur: Government Press, 1954. No. 9 of 1954. "Establishment of a Public Service Commission."

——. ——. First Session. *Proceedings.* Kuala Lumpur: Government Press, 1951. Council Paper No. 13 of 1948. "Report of the Joint Committee on Cost of Living Allowances."

——. ——. Third Session. *Proceedings.* Kuala Lumpur: Government Press, 1953.

——. ——. Fifth Session. *Proceedings.* Kuala Lumpur: Government Press, 1953.

——. ——. Eighth Session. *Proceedings.* Kuala Lumpur: Government Press, 1956.

——. SECOND LEGISLATIVE COUNCIL. Third Session. *Debates.* Kuala Lumpur: Government Press, 1958.

——. ——. Fourth Session. *Debates.* Kuala Lumpur: Government Press, 1959.

——. ——. First Session. *Minutes and Council Papers.* Kuala Lumpur: Government Press, 1957. No. 6 of 1956. "Report of the Federation of Malaya Constitutional Conference Held in London in January and February 1956."

MALAYAN UNION. ADVISORY COUNCIL. *Proceedings, 1946.* Kuala Lumpur: Government Press, 1948. Council Paper No. 36 of 1946. "Memorandum on Interim Joint Council."

F. *Financial Estimates*

FEDERATION OF MALAYA. *Estimates of Federal Ordinary Expenditures for the Year 1960.* Kuala Lumpur: Government Press, 1959.

——. *Estimates of the Federal Revenue and Expenditure for the Year 1960.* Kuala Lumpur: Government Press, 1959.

————. State of Johore. *Estimates of Revenue and Expenditure for the Year 1960.* Johore Bahru: Johore Government Printing Office, 1959.

————. State of Kedah. *Estimates of Revenue and Expenditure for the Year 1960.* Alor Star: Kedah Government Press, 1959.

————. State of Kelantan. *Estimates of Revenue and Expenditure for the Year 1960.* Kuala Lumpur: Government Press, 1960.

————. State of Malacca. *Estimates of Revenue and Expenditure for the Year 1960.* Kuala Lumpur: Government Press, 1960.

————. State of Negri Sembilan. *Estimates of the Revenue and Expenditure for the Year 1960.* Kuala Lumpur: Government Press, 1959.

————. State of Pahang. *Estimates of the Revenue and Expenditure for the Year 1960.* Kuala Lumpur: Government Press, 1960.

————. State of Penang. *Estimates of the Revenue and Expenditure for the Year 1960.* Kuala Lumpur: Government Press, 1959.

————. State of Perak. *Estimates of Revenue and Expenditure for the Year 1960.* Kuala Lumpur: Government Press, 1960.

————. State of Perlis. *Estimates of the Revenue and Expenditure for the Period 3rd Rajab, 1379 to 13th Rajab, 1380, as Covered by the Year 1960.* Alor Star: Kedah Government Press, 1959.

————. State of Selangor. *Estimates of Revenue and Expenditure for the Year 1960.* Kuala Lumpur: Government Press, 1959.

————. State of Trengganu. *Estimates of the Revenue and Expenditure for the Year 1960.* Kuala Trengganu: Trengganu Government Press, 1959.

————. *Estimates of Revenue and Expenditure 1st January to 31st December 1961.* Kuala Lumpur: Government Press, 1961.

G. *State and Federal Enactments*

FEDERATED MALAY STATES. *The Laws of the Federated Malay States, 1935.* London: C. F. Roworth, Ltd., 1935.

————. *Supplement to the Laws of the Federated Malay States.* Kuala Lumpur: Government Press, 1939 with insertions covering 1940.

FEDERATION OF MALAYA. *Malayan Union and Federal Ordinances and State and Settlement Enactments Passed During the Year 1948.* Kuala Lumpur: Government Press, 1950. No. 7. "Interpretation and General Clauses Ordinance, 1948."

————. ————. No. 19. "Public Authorities Protection Ordinance, 1948."

————. ————. No. 43. "The Courts Ordinance, 1948."

————. *Federal Ordinances and State and Settlement Enactments, 1949.* Kuala Lumpur: Government Press, 1950. No. 4. "Trade Disputes Ordinance, 1949."

————. ————. No. 67. "Government Contracts Ordinance, 1949."

————. *Federal Ordinances and State and Settlement Enactments, 1950*. Kuala Lumpur: Government Press, 1951. No. 5. "Prevention of Corruption Ordinance, 1950."

————. ————. No. 11. "The Evidence Ordinance, 1950."

————. ————. No. 14. "The Contracts (Malay States) Ordinance."

————. ————. No. 52. "Local Authorities Election Ordinance, 1950."

————. ————. No. 75. "Widows and Orphans Pensions."

————. *Federal Ordinances and State and Settlement Enactments, 1951*. Kuala Lumpur: Government Press, 1952. No. 1. "The Pensions Ordinance, 1951."

————. ————. No. 21. "The Employees' Provident Fund Ordinance, 1951."

————. *Federal Ordinances and State and Settlement Enactments, 1952*. Kuala Lumpur: Government Press, 1953. No. 14. "The Police Ordinance. 1952."

————. ————. No. 36. "Land Council Ordinance, 1952."

————. *Federal Ordinances and State and Settlement Enactments, 1954*. Kuala Lumpur: Government Press, 1956. No. 9. "The Election Offences Ordinance. 1954."

————. *Federal Ordinances and State and Settlement Enactments, 1955*. Kuala Lumpur: Government Press, 1957. No. 34. "Small Estates (Distribution) Ordinance. 1955."

————. ————. No. 38. "Employment Ordinance, 1955."

————. *Federal Ordinances and State and Settlement Enactments, 1956*. Kuala Lumpur: Government Press, 1958. No. 17. "Pensions (Entitled Officers) Ordinance. 1956."

————. ————. No. 21. "Entitled Officers (Gratuities) Ordinance, 1956."

————. ————. No. 43. "Employment (Amendment) Ordinance, 1956."

————. ————. No. 56. "Delegation of Powers Ordinance, 1956."

————. ————. No. 59. "The Federation of Malaya Agreement (Amendment No. 4) Ordinance, 1956."

————. *Federal Ordinances and State and Settlement Enactments, 1957*. Kuala Lumpur: Government Press, 1959. No. 28. "Pensions (Entitled Officers) and Entitled Officers (Gratuities) (Repeal) Ordinance, 1957."

————. ————. No. 60. "The Audit Ordinance, 1957."

————. ————. No. 62. "Financial Procedures Ordinance, 1957."

————. ————. No. 74. "The Service Commissions Ordinance, 1957."

————. *Federal Ordinances and State Enactments, 1958*. Kuala Lumpur: Government Press, 1959. No. 28. "The Widows and Orphans Pension (Amendment) Ordinance. 1958."

————. ————. Pahang No. 9. "Public Services Commission (Extension of Jurisdiction) Enactment, 1958."

————. ————. Perlis No. 7. "Public Services Commission (Extension of Jurisdiction) Enactment, 1958."

————. State of Negri Sembilan. *Public Services Commission (Extension of Jurisdiction)* Enactment, 1959. Kuala Lumpur: Government Press, 1959.

————. *Subsidiary Legislation, 1947.* Kuala Lumpur: Government Press, 1951. L. N. 2130. "Labour Union Participation by Government Employees."

————. ————. L. N. 4103. "Participation in Labour Unions."

————. *Federal Subsidiary Legislation, 1958.* Kuala Lumpur: Government Press, 1959. L. N. 329. "Federal Capital (Municipal Elections) (Conduct of Elections) Regulations, 1958."

MALAYAN UNION. *Ordinances Passed during the Year 1946.* Kuala Lumpur: Government Press, 1949. No. 12. "Trade Union Ordinance. 1946."

H. *Staff Lists and Service Schemes*

FEDERATED MALAY STATES. *Civil Service List, 1913.* Kuala Lumpur: Government Press, 1913.

————. *Civil List, 1918.* Kuala Lumpur: Government Press, 1918.

————. *Conditions of Service and Salary Schemes for Officers on the Malayan Establishment.* Kuala Lumpur: Government Press, 1937.

————. *The Malay Administrative Service List, 1931.* Kuala Lumpur: Government Press, 1931.

————. *Malay Administrative Service List, 1940.* Kuala Lumpur: Government Press, 1940.

————. *Reprint of Salary Schemes (Locally Recruited Officers).* Kuala Lumpur: Government Press, 1940.

FEDERATED MALAY STATES AND SINGAPORE. *Malayan Establishment: Agreement, Conditions of Service and Salary Schemes.* Title page missing.

FEDERATION OF MALAYA. *Malayan Civil Service List, 1st July 1959.* Kuala Lumpur: Government Press, 1959.

————. *Malayan Civil Service List, 1st January 1960.* Kuala Lumpur: Government Press, 1960.

————. *Malayan Civil Service List, 1st January 1961.* Kuala Lumpur: Government Press, 1961.

————. *Malayan Civil Service List, 1st January 1962.* Kuala Lumpur: Government Press, 1962.

————. *Scheme of Service, Malay Administrative Service, 1954.* Kuala Lumpur: mimeographed, 1954.

————. *Schemes of Service, 1950.* Kuala Lumpur: Government Press, 1950.

————. *Schemes of Service, 1956.* Kuala Lumpur: Government Press, issued at irregular intervals after 1956. Vol. I.

————. *Schemes of Service.* Kuala Lumpur: Government Press, issued at irregular intervals after 1958. Vol. II.

————. *Staff List, 1st January 1957.* Kuala Lumpur: Government Press, 1957.

————. *Staff List, 1st January 1958.* Kuala Lumpur: Government Press, 1958.

————. *Staff List, 1st January 1959.* Kuala Lumpur: Government Press, 1959.

————. *Staff List, 1st January 1960.* Kuala Lumpur: Government Press, 1960.

————. *Staff List, 1st January 1961.* Kuala Lumpur: Government Press, 1961.

————. *Staff List, 1st January 1962.* Kuala Lumpur: Government Press, 1962.

MALAYAN UNION. *Malayan Establishment List, 31st December 1947.* Kuala Lumpur: Government Press, 1948.

STRAITS SETTLEMENTS AND FEDERATED MALAY STATES. *The Malayan Civil List, 1940.* Singapore: Government Printing Office, 1940.

————. *Malayan Establishment List as on 1st July, 1941.* Singapore: Government Printing Office, 1941.

I. *Miscellaneous*

FEDERATED MALAY STATES. *Correspondence Respecting the Federation of the Protected Malay States.* Taiping, Perak: Perak Government Printing Office, 1896.

————. *Government Gazette.* September 9, 1921. Kuala Lumpur: Government Press, 1921.

————. *Yearbook, 1924.* Kuala Lumpur: Government Press, 1924.

————. *Yearbook, 1930.* Kuala Lumpur: Government Press, 1930.

FEDERATION OF MALAYA. *An Act to Amend the Constitution of the Federation.* Kuala Lumpur: Government Press, 1960.

————. *Agreement for the Constitution of a Federation Establishment.* Kuala Lumpur: Government Press, 1956.

————. *Constitution of the Whitley Council for Divisions I–IV of the Public Services of the Federation of Malaya as Amended.* Kuala Lumpur: mimeographed, n.d.

————. *Constitutional Proposals.* Kuala Lumpur: Government Press, 1957.

————. *The Federation of Malaya Agreement, 1948.* Kuala Lumpur: Government Press, 1948 and 1956.

————. *The Federation of Malaya and United Kingdom Public Officers Agreement, 1959.* Kuala Lumpur: Government Press, 1959.

————. *General Orders.* Kuala Lumpur: Government Press, amendments and new chapters issued at irregular intervals after 1958.

————. *Malayan Constitutional Documents.* Second Edition. Kuala Lumpur: Government Press, 1962. Vol. I.

————. *Malayan Establishment Agreement.* Kuala Lumpur: Government Press, 1948.

————. *The Pensions Ordinance, 1951.* Kuala Lumpur: Government Press, 1951.

————. *The Police Ordinance, 1952.* Kuala Lumpur: Government Press, reprinted 1959.

————. *Police Regulations.* Kuala Lumpur: Government Press, 1959.

————. *Rules of the Supreme Court.* Kuala Lumpur: Government Press, 1957.

————. *Service in the Government of the Federation of Malaya.* Kuala Lumpur: Government Press, 1957.

————. Penang High Court. Civil Suit No. 232 of 1959. *Surinder Singh Kanda v. the Government of the Federation of Malaya.* Penang: typescript, 1960.

————. Supreme Court of the Federation of Malaya in the Court of Appeal at Kuala Lumpur. F. M. Civil Appeal No. 30 of 1960. *The Government of the Federation of Malaya v. B. Surinder Singh Kanda.* Kuala Lumpur: mimeographed, 1961. Three separate opinions.

————. Supreme Court of the Federation of Malay in the High Court at Kuala Lumpur. Originating Motions No. 2 of 1959 and 3 of 1959. *Rasiah Munusamy v. The Public Services Commission.* Kuala Lumpur: typescript, 1960.

MALAYAN UNION. *Government Gazette.* December 24, 1946. Kuala Lumpur: Government Press, 1946.

SINGAPORE. *Annual Report, 1958.* Singapore: Government Printing Office, 1959.

UNIVERSITY OF MALAYA. *Calendar, 1960–1.* Singapore: Straits Times (Malaya) Ltd., 1960.

II. United Kingdom

GREAT BRITAIN. *Rules and Orders, 1946.* London: His Majesty's Stationery Office, 1947. Vol. I.

————. *Statutory Instruments, 1948.* London: His Majesty's Stationery Office, 1949. Vol. I. Part 1.

————. Colonial Office, *Federation of Malaya.* London: His Majesty's Stationery Office, 1947.

———. ———. MacMichael, Sir Harold. *Report on a Mission to Malaya.* London: His Majesty's Stationery Office, 1946.

———. ———. *Malayan Union and Singapore: Statement of Policy on Future Constitution.* London: His Majesty's Stationery Office, 1946.

———. ———. *Organization of the Colonial Service.* London: His Majesty's Stationery Office, 1946.

———. ———. *Reorganization of the Colonial Service.* London: Her Majesty's Stationery Office, 1954.

———. ———. *Report of the Federation of Malaya Constitutional Commission, 1957.* London: Her Majesty's Stationery Office, 1957.

———. House of Commons. *Debates, 1833.* London: T. C. Hansard, 1833. Vol. XIX.

———. ———. *Debates, 1945/46.* Second Session. London: His Majesty's Stationery Office, 1945. Vol. 414.

———. ———. *Sessional Papers, 1857/58.* London: Her Majesty's Stationery Office, 1858. Vol. II.

———. ———. *Sessional Papers, 1862.* London: Her Majesty's Stationery Office, 1862. Vol. XL.

———. ———. *Accounts and Papers, 1917–1918.* London: His Majesty's Stationery Office, 1918. Vol. XVIII.

———. ———. *Sessional Papers, 1866.* London: Her Majesty's Stationery Office, 1866. Vols. III, V.

———. ———. *Sessional Papers, 1929–30.* London: His Majesty's Stationery Office, 1930. Vols. VIII, IX.

———. Supreme Allied Command, South East Asia. *Report on the British Military Administration of Malaya.* Kuala Lumpur: Government Press, 1946.

Index

Abdul Aziz bin Haji Abdul Majid, Dato, vi
Abdul Rahman, Tengku, 132
Allen, G. C., 22 n., 52 n., 53 n.
Almond, Gabriel A., 4 n., 117 n.
Apter, David, 5 n.
Atkinson, G. A., 90 n.
Auber, Peter, 38 n.

Banner, Hubert A., 59 n.
Basham, A. L., 7 n., 15 n.
Birch, J. W. W., 26 n.
Blunt, Sir Edward, 40
Braibanti, Ralph, vii, 5, 87 n., 96 n., 107 n., 129 n.
Briggs Plan, 34
Brimmell, J. H., 29 n.
British Association of Malaya, 32 n.
British Military Administration (BMA), 108
Brown, C. C., 6 n., 9 n.
Bucknill, Sir John A. S., 46 n.
Bureaucratic organization, 82-101; degree of achievement orientation, 125-129; degree of rationality, 129-132; degree of structural differentiation, 122-125; internal administration, 90-101; salaries and perquisites, 88-90; size, 84-88; Whitley Councils, 97-100

Campbell, Arthur, 29 n.
Chapman, F. Spencer, 32 n.
Cheeseman, H. R., 7 n.
Chinese community: attitude toward Malayan Union, 34 n.; and colonial education policies, 59-60; economic roles, 23; and Emergency, 29-35; literacy, 19-20; and Malayanization, 70-76; population, 16-19; relations with colonial power, 27-30; religions, 20-21
Clementi, Sir Cecil, 33 n.
Clifford, Sir Hugh, 44 n.
Cobbold Commission, 133 n.
Coédes, George, 6 n.

Cole, R. Taylor, vii, 110 n.
Coleman, James S., 4 n., 117 n.
Colonial services, 37-62, 82-84, 100-101, 108-109, 111-114, 116-117, 122-132 passim, 134; Malayanization of, 63-81
Colonialism and colonial policies in Malaya: Colonial Office period, 45-62; and colonial services, 46-49; and communal separatism, 26-31; and Company civil service, 40-44; demise of Company, 44-45; development of communications, 53-58; and economic development, 49-53; and education, 58-60; and English East India Company, 37-45; origins of, 39-40
Comber, Leon, 27 n.
Communities: recruitment quotas, 81, 96, 110 n.; representation in bureaucracy, 69-76; representation in Malayan society, 16-19. See also Chinese, Indian, Malay communities
Congress of Unions of Employees in the Public and Civil Services (CUEPACS), 98 n., 99 n.
Cowan, C. D., 6 n.

Dartford, G. P., 27 n.
Davidson, J. H., 27 n.
Dawood, N. J., 24 n.
Donnithorne, Audrey G., 22 n., 52 n., 53 n.
Dull, Paul S., 80 n.

Emergency in Malaya (1948-60), 28-36, 118
Emerson, Rupert, 49
English East India Company, 37-45 passim

Federation Establishment Office (FEO). See Bureaucratic organization: internal administration
Fisher, C. A., 54, 62 n.
Fisher, Warren, 47 n., 48

Gent, Sir Edward, 32 n.
Gibson, William Sumner, 47 n.
Ginsburg, Norton, 17 n.
Gullick, J. M., vii, 6 n., 7 n., 8 n., 9 n., 12 n., 15 n., 44 n.

Haimes, W. J., 97, 97 n., 99
Hall, D. G. E., 6 n., 39 n.
Hamzah bin Abdullah, Dato, vi
Harbison, Frederick, 110
Harrison, Brian, 58 n.
Hawkins, Gerald, 34 n.
Hayes, C. J., 95 n.
Heine-Geldern, Robert, 10 n., 11 n., 14, 14 n.
Henderson, A. M., 13 n.
Ho Seng Ong, 59 n.
Holman, Dennis, 32 n.
Hooker, Sir Joseph, 52
Hoover, Calvin B., 21 n.
Howitt, C. R., vi

Ibbetson, Sir Denzil, 10
Ike, Nobutaka, 80 n.
Indian community: attitude toward Malayan Union, 34 n.; and colonial education policies, 60; economic roles, 23; and Emergency, 31; literacy, 20; and Malayanization, 69-76 *passim*; population, 16-19; relations with colonial power, 31; religion, 21
Indian Immigration Fund, 31

Jeffries, Sir Charles, 48 n.
Jones, S. W., 60 n.
Judicial and Legal Service Commission. *See* Bureaucratic organization: internal administration

Kanda, Surinder Singh, 96 n.
Kennedy, J., 6 n.

Land Administration Commission, 24, 118 n.
LaPalombara, Joseph, 50 n., 96 n., 121-122 n., 125 n., 131
Lee Kuan Yew, 22 n.
Lerner, Daniel, 4 n.
Lewis, W. Arthur, 50 n.
Light, Francis, 39
Low, Sir Hugh, 27 n.
Lugard, Lord, 57 n.

MacMichael, Sir Harold, 32 n.
Maine, Sir Henry, 4 n.
Malay Administrative Service (MAS), 102-120, 63, 82 n.; socialization function, 111-114
Malay College, 76, 111-112, 127

Malay community: attitude toward Malayan Union, 33 n.; and colonial education policies, 60; economic roles, 23; and Emergency, 30-31; literacy, 19-20; and Malayanization, 70-76; population, 16-19; relations with colonial power, 26-27; religion, 20
Malay Reservations, 25
Malayan Civil Service (MCS), 102-120; communal composition of, 68-69, 109-111; contemporary character of, 107-114; degree of achievement orientation, 127; origin of title, 46 n.; as political elite, 117-120; and political process, 115-120; position in bureaucratic hierarchy, 102-104; recruitment quotas to, 81, 110, 110 n.; relation to Indian Civil Service, 104-107
Malayan Communist Party (MCP), 30, 32 n., 34 n.
Malayan Peoples Anti-Japanese Army (MPAJA), 32, 34
Malayan Peoples Anti-Japanese Union (MPAJU), 32
Malayan Planning Unit (MPU), 32 n.
Malayan Union, 32-34 n.
Malayanization, 63-81; complications of, 77-81; origins and provisions of, 63-68; statistical results of, 68-76
Malaysia, Federation of, 132-137
Mann, A. R., vi
Markham, Sir Clements, 52
MAS. *See* Malay Administrative Service
Maxwell, Sir George, 32-33 n., 46 n., 47 n.
MCP. *See* Malayan Communist Party
MCS. *See* Malayan Civil Service
Mohamed Rashid, Inche, 93 n.
Moorhead, F. J., 6 n.
MPAJA. *See* Malayan Peoples Anti-Japanese Army
MPAJU. *See* Malayan Peoples Anti-Japanese Union
Munusamy, Rashia v. The Public Services Commission, 96 n.

National Land Council, 24 n.
Ng Sien Yoong, 28 n.
Northrop, F. S. C., 14 n., 79

Onn bin Jafa'ar, Dato, 33 n.

Pan-Malayan Islamic Party, 36, 62
Parkinson, C. Northcote, 27 n.
Parsons, Talcott, 13 n.
Pauker, Guy J., 79 n.
Pearson, Aylmer C., 31 n.
Philips, C. H., 38 n.

Pires, Tomé, 6 n.
Plural society in Malaya: communal, 16-19; economic, 21-25; linguistic, 19-20; religious, 20-21
PMIP. *See* Pan-Malayan Islamic Party
Principal Establishment Officer (PEO). *See* Bureaucratic organization: internal administration
Public Service Appointments and Promotions Board (PSAPB), 93-94
Public Services Commission (PSC), 66, 91; judicial appeal from decisions of, 96. *See also* Bureaucratic organization: internal administration
Purcell, Victor, 28 n., 29 n., 34 n., 44 n.
Pye, Lucian W., 4 n., 5, 28 n., 30 n., 32 n., 34 n., 116, 117 n.

Raffles, Sir Stamford, 40 n., 43, 44 n.
Railway Service Commission. *See* Bureaucratic organization: internal administration
Redfield, Robert, 4 n.
Ridley, H. N. "Rubber," 52-53 n.
Riggs, Fred W., 4 n., 5, 5 n., 125 n.
Roberts, Chester F., 17 n.
Robinson, J. B. Perry, 29 n.

Sharkey, Lawrence, 34 n.
Sharpley, Cecil H., 34 n.
Silcock, T. H., vii, 21, 25 n., 34
Skeat, Walter William, 10 n., 11, 13 n.
Soedjatmoko, 79 n.
Spengler, Joseph J., 5 n., 50 n., 87 n., 129 n.
Swettenham, Sir Frank, 33 n., 44 n.

Tan Siew Sin, 110 n.
Taylor Commission, 88
Templer, General Sir Gerald, 28-29 n., 35
Thayer, Philip W., 79 n.
Tönnies, Ferdinand, 4 n.
Tradition and traditional systems in Malaya: abstraction of term, 4-5; ascriptive nature of, 7-10; cosmological principles of, 14-15; history and sources, 6-7; and influence on contemporary bureaucracy, 79-81, 88; religion and magic in, 10-13; sources of authority, 13-15
Treacher, W. H., 49
Treaty of Federation (1896), 46-47 n.
Treaty of Pangkor (1874), 27, 46 n., 50
Tregonning, K. G., 38 n.
Trusted, Sir Harry, 84 n.

Wang Gunwu, 111 n.
Ward, Robert E., 80 n.
Warren Fisher Committee, 47 n., 48
Watherston, Sir David, vii
Weber, Max, 4 n., 13 n.
Whitley, J. H., 97 n.
Whitleyism and Whitley Councils, 97-100
Wilkinson, R. J., 8 n., 12 n.
Wilson, Sir Samuel, 32 n.
Winstedt, Sir Richard O., 6, 6 n., 9 n., 11 n., 12, 12 n., 13 n., 14 n., 15 n., 33 n., 44 n.